Campaign for change Toolkit

Acknowledgements

Written by:
Fiona Mcgee

With Thanks to:
The Campaign Company:
Matthew Upton
Dani Parry
Nancy Platts
Dan Maxon

UK Youth:
Emma McEwan
Carola Adams
Yvonne Richards

UKYP and Unite Participation

Contributors
UK Youth Voice
Acorns Children's Hospice
Shropshire Care Crew Council
Durham Young Gay People Network
Fredrick Street Youth Centre
LGYM – Lesbian and Gay Youth Manchester
Nancherrow Youth Centre
North Tyneside Children in Care Council
Project 28
Right Track National Initiative
BIET's
Speaking Up Youth Parliament, Nottingham
Warrington Youth Club
YMCA Darlington
YWCA Kirkby
YWCA London West
YWCA West Kent

For further information please contact:
UK Youth
Avon Tyrrell
Bransgore
Hampshire
BH23 8EE

Tel: 01425 672 347
Fax: 01425 675 108
Email: info@ukyouth.org
Website:
www.ukyouthhearingunheardvoices.org
www.ukyouth.org

Designed by:
Adept Design
www.adeptdesign.co.uk

All rights reserved. This publication is copyright but may be reproduced on a small scale for educational and training purposes only by any method without fee or prior permission, subject to the inclusion of the following words: 'taken from Campaign Challenge Toolkit' copyright UK Youth 2009.'

Large-scale reproduction or inclusion of extracts in publications for sale may be done only with prior written permission from UK Youth and fee may be payable.

While all reasonable care has been taken in the compilation and editing of this publication, UK Youth shall not be liable for any loss, howsoever arising, which is occasioned to any person who places reliance upon any editorial material and in particular (but without limitation) for any loss occasioned by factual changes which have occurred since this publication went to press.

Funded through BIG Lottery Fund

CONTENTS

Introduction — 5-6

UK Youth
Hearing Unheard Voices
Campaign for Change
Youth Challenges and Youth Achievement Awards
Overview of Campaign for Change Contents

Information Sheets — 7-34

Planning It
1. What is a Campaign?
2. Getting Started
3. Knowing What You Want
4. What's Your Campaign Message?
5. Knowing Who To Influence
6. Building Your Case
7. Evidence Gathering
8. Planning Your Campaign
9. Coming Up With An Action Plan
10. Building A Team
11. Evaluating Your Campaign
12. How to Evaluate Your Campaign

Doing It
A. Campaign Checklist
B. Campaigning Action Tools: visual, written word, performance, social media, spoken word
C. Raising Awareness
D. Some Do's and Don'ts of Campaigning
E. Get Lobbying
F. Get Writing
G. Face to face meetings
H. Shout About It!
I. Contacting Journalists
J. Writing Press Releases
K. Working with Third Party Endorsements
L. Public Speaking
M. Planning a Presentation
N. Negotiation Skills
O. Making Meetings Work

Session Plans and Activity Sheets — 35-66

Session Plans
1. What is a campaign?
2. Getting Your Voice Heard
3. Have Your Say
4. Defining the Issue
5. Choosing a Campaign Goal
6. Choosing Who To Focus On
7. Debating the Issue
8. Balloon Exercise
9. Deciding on your Message
10. What Makes a Good Slogan?
11. £5 note exercise
12. Steps to the Future
13. Planning a Campaign
14. Action Planning
15. Team building
16. What I Want to Achieve
17. Lobbying Exercises
18. Dealing with the Media
19. Negotiating and Influencing
20. Practicing Public Speaking
21. Running a Public Meeting
22. Setting up a Facebook Group or Page
23. Setting up a Twitter Feed
24. Starting a Blog
25. Creating an Online Survey

Activity Sheets
1A. What is a campaign?
3A. Debating topics
4A. Defining the Issue
6A. Influence Map
8A. Balloon Template
12A. Footprints Template
13A. Planning a Campaign Scenario
14A. Action Plan Pro-Forma
14B. SWOT Analysis
16A. What I Want to Achieve Pro-Forma
18A. Selling In Exercise
18B. Writing a Press Release
19A. Negotiating Skills Sheet
19B. How should the Council spend its money?
20A. Planning Your Presentation
Evaluation Pro-Forma

Challenges and Targets — 67-74

1. Introduction to accrediting campaigning
2. Planning a campaign
3. Doing It
4. Shout About It

Accreditation — 75-84

UK Youth's Challenges and Achievement Awards
Levels
Structure of the Awards
Recording the Process
Delivering the Youth Achievement Awards
Using the Youth Challenges and Youth Achievement Awards in a Formal Education Setting
Links to Other Awards and Qualifications

Additional Information — 85-99

Campaigning in Context
Data Protection
Contacting politicians
Lobbying Local Government
Lobbying MPs
Public Protests and the Law
The Campaigner's Dictionary
Where to go for further support

INTRODUCTION

UK Youth

UK Youth is a national charity developing and promoting innovative non-formal educational programmes and opportunities for and with young people, in order to develop their full potential.

It is the leading national youth work charity supporting over 750,000 young people, helping them to raise their aspirations, realise their potential and have their achievements recognised via non-formal, accredited education programmes and activities.

UK Youth works to support and enable young people to become actively involved citizens through taking responsibility for their own learning and the learning of others.

For more information go to: www.ukyouth.org

Hearing Unheard Voices

This Campaign for Change toolkit is part of UK Youth's Hearing Unheard Voices Project and is funded by the Big Lottery Fund.

Hearing Unheard Voices aims to give disadvantaged young people the skills and opportunities to speak up to shape their services, using media and campaigning activities.

Campaign for Change

This toolkit is intended as a practical resource for anyone working with young people aged 11-19 involved in campaigning activities at any level.

It aims to:

- Equip young people and anyone working with them to run and review local, regional and national campaigns to influence young people's services
- Support anyone working with young people to accredit local, regional and national media campaigns through the Youth Challenges and the Youth Achievement Awards
- Highlight examples of existing good practice

The materials contained within the pack are designed to:

- Increase understanding of what makes a strong campaign
- Offer practical suggestions for challenges and targets to support the development of campaigns
- Look at where things may go wrong and how this can be avoided

Youth Challenges and Youth Achievement Awards

The Youth Challenges and Youth Achievement Awards are a flexible framework for accrediting the engagement and learning of children and young people aged 11-25. They are a peer-assessed portfolio based learning framework for young people that is accredited to national standards by ASDAN. Further information about the Awards can be found in the Accrediting What You Do section of this toolkit.

Designed to work within the framework of the Youth Achievement Awards, this toolkit is also a stand-alone resource, containing adaptable ideas and activities for use within structured non-formal education programmes as well as the formal classroom environment.

INTRODUCTION

Overview of Campaign for Change Contents

Information Sheets

The Information Sheets in the toolkit are designed to promote learning and enable young people to get the most out of their involvement in campaigning. The sheets have been divided into two sections:

- Planning It   (page 8)
- Doing It   (page 16)

They can be photocopied and used as handouts.

Challenges and Targets

There are many different kinds of activities and programmes that can be used as part of the campaigning process and which can be accredited via the Youth Challenges and Youth Achievement Awards. This section makes suggestions for activities in 4 areas:

- Introduction to accrediting campaigning   (page 68)
- Planning a campaign   (page 69)
- Doing It   (page 71)
- Shout About It   (page 74)

The material contained here has been designed to be used flexibly, but workers and young people can also design their own challenges. These could be based on local priorities, young people's needs and interests, or in response to issues that arise in young people's lives.

Session Plans and Activity Sheets

This section of the toolkit contains a variety of session plans and activity sheets that are linked to the activities, challenges and targets. They can be adapted to suit the particular needs of a group. They are designed to offer practical tools to enable young people to define, plan and carry out their campaign.

Accreditation

This section gives detailed information on the structure and process of running the Youth Challenges and Youth Achievement Awards. It also covers the guidelines for portfolio evidence collection.

For those working with young people in a formal education setting, this section also gives details on the links between campaigning activities and the PSHE / Citizenship curriculum.

This section also includes links with other accreditation schemes.

5. Additional information

This section of the toolkit contains additional information on a number of aspects of campaigning:

- Campaigning in Context   (page 85)
- Data Protection   (page 86)
- Contacting politicians   (page 87)
- Lobbying Local Government   (page 88)
- Lobbying MPs   (page 89)
- Public Protests and the Law   (page 91)
- The Campaigner's Dictionary   (page 92)
- Where to go for further support   (page 96)

ukyouth Hearing Unheard Voices

INFORMATION SHEETS

Introduction

Most people would say that there are things in the world they would like to see change. You may sometimes have found yourself thinking "well, that's not right, shouldn't someone be doing something about this?", but perhaps you haven't had the confidence to think that that person should, in fact, be YOU.

So, if you and your friends have decided there's something you want to take action about and you really want to get on with it, then the information contained here is designed to help you do this.

There are 27 information sheets here, which are divided into two sections:

▷ Planning It

▷ Doing It

The sheets have been designed to be used flexibly, so that you can choose the most appropriate combination of sheets for your particular group. It is not necessary to use all the sheets in sequence from 1 to 26.

Planning It

This section covers some of the basics, such as what is a campaign, before going on to look at what makes a campaign work and suggest ways to help you plan your campaign in easy stages.

Doing It

This section offers practical tips and suggestions to help you get on with the process of actually running your campaign. It looks at the different methods you can use, as well as providing some handy hints and suggestions as to how best to go about getting what you want.

Contents

Planning It
1. What is a Campaign? — 8
2. Getting Started — 10
3. Knowing What You Want — 10
4. What's Your Campaign Message? — 11
5. Knowing Who To Influence — 11
6. Building Your Case — 12
7. Evidence Gathering — 13
8. Planning Your Campaign — 13
9. Coming Up With An Action Plan — 14
10. Building A Team — 16
11. Evaluating Your Campaign — 16
12. How to Evaluate Your Campaign — 17

Doing It
A. Campaign Checklist — 18
B. Campaigning Action Tools: visual, written word, performance, social media, spoken word — 18
C. Raising Awareness — 24
D. Some Do's and Don'ts of Campaigning — 24
E. Get Lobbying — 26
F. Get Writing — 26
G. Face to face meetings — 27
H. Shout About It! — 27
I. Contacting Journalists — 29
J. Writing Press Releases — 29
K. Working with Third Party Endorsements — 30
L. Public Speaking — 31
M. Planning a Presentation — 32
N. Negotiation Skills — 32
O. Making Meetings Work — 33

Case Studies
Sex and Relationships Education Campaign — 9
Lesbian and Gay Youth Manchester — 15
Jeans for Genes — 25
Right Track — 28
UK Youth Voice — 34

INFORMATION SHEETS

PLANNING IT

1. What is a campaign?

"Organised actions around a specific issue seeking to bring about changes in the policy and behaviours of institutions and / or specific public groups."

Chances are that you have already been involved in a number of campaigns before, even if you don't think you have. Anyone who has ever voted in X-Factor or Big Brother, worn a ribbon or a wristband to mark something, signed a petition or joined a facebook group is actually taking part in a campaign.

In short, a campaign is usually about getting the people with power to make the decisions you want, or getting other people to collectively behave differently to improve things. It is about persuading others that not only are you right, but that you are so right they must take some form of action.

Campaigns are usually made up of a series of co-ordinated activities, such as speeches and petitions, designed to inform and convince people of a particular cause or to influence their decisions by persuasive techniques.

Campaigns have an important role to play in our society, because they focus on the right of the individual to make his / her voice heard. Young people are a group whose opinions are often ignored or overlooked. Campaigns can therefore be of particular importance to young people, because they offer the opportunity to make real improvements in their own lives and those of the others around them.

People run campaigns about all kinds of things, from something really local right through to national and international issues. For example, a local campaign might be about trying to improve a playground in your local community, or getting nicer toilet paper in the loos in your school; at a national level, you might want to join a campaign asking the government to change something (for example, get rid of university tuition fees, or do more to end child poverty). At an international level, people from different countries might campaign together on issues like banning seal clubbing or stopping the war in Afghanistan.

Whatever the issue, there are usually two main reasons that people decide to campaign:

▷ To create awareness about an issue amongst the general public or a specific audience

And / or

▷ To influence or change a decision or policy

If there's something that you feel passionate about, something that you feel should be improved or changed, then you've got a campaign just waiting to be planned and carried out. So get together with your friends, and get cracking.

You might want to check out session plan 1 page 36

Sex and Relationships Education Campaign

Are you getting it? This simple question was posed by the Members of the UK Youth Parliament (UKYP) to over 20,000 young people. It spearheaded a national campaign to ensure that all young people had access to consistent, high quality sex and relationships education (SRE) throughout the UK.

Too little, too late, too biological and little, if any, information on relationships – that is what Members of the Youth Parliament (MYPs) had been saying about their SRE since 2001. In 2007 they set about proving it. They went to extraordinary lengths to canvass the opinions of over 21,000 young people from across the country in a survey entirely designed, produced and sent out by young people. Shockingly, they found that over half of young people had never been taught about teenage pregnancy, wouldn't know where to find their local sexual health clinic and had not been taught how to use a condom.

Shout About It

The UK Youth Parliament knew that these were damning figures and that they had to act on them. To make sure the Government really did listen, they knew they had to get a huge amount of publicity. In October they drafted a letter to a national newspaper, calling on the Government to listen to the voices of those 21,000 young people. Over 100 leading sexual health organisations, Primary Care Trusts, children's charities, teaching unions and celebrities signed up to the letter.

The UK Youth Parliament figures and the letter made the front page of The Times in a week where media attention was already focused on sexually transmitted infections and the rise in teenage pregnancy. It clearly resonated throughout the UK and led to blanket national and local press coverage.

Bolstered by the publicity their campaign had attracted, MYPs met with Jim Knight, Schools Minister on 6th December. They left the Minister in no doubt of the strength of feeling by young people. After meeting with the Minister, MYPs continued their publicity onslaught with appearances on national television and radio, as well as local print interviews.

Campaign for Change

Astonishingly, in early 2008 the Government announced a review of the current provision of sex and relationships education across the UK. Significantly for the UK Youth Parliament, an MYP was asked to co-chair the review, ensuring that young people's voices really are heard on this vital issue. And as a result of that review, sex and relationships education is going to be made compulsory in both primary and secondary schools.

Now, young people will finally have the chance to say, "Yes, I'm getting it!"

INFORMATION SHEETS

You might want to check out session plan 4 page 38

You might want to check out session plan 5 page 40

2. Getting Started

People talk about things that could be turned into campaigns all the time. If you've ever had a conversation with your friends about something that you all want to change or an issue that you wish more people would take notice of, then you've got the beginnings of your campaign right there. What you need to do next is ask yourself some key questions which will really help you to focus on what exactly your campaign should be.

Getting Focussed

Some of the key questions you will need to answer to make sure you have a strong plan in place include:

- What is the problem as you see it at the moment?
- What needs to change for your position to be adopted or become reality?
- What arguments can you make to support your position?
- Are your arguments well researched and persuasive to the people you want to influence?
- Are you alone or do you think this issue will affect lots of people?
- Who are the opposition and what are their arguments?
- What evidence will work best to support your arguments?
- What does the person or organisation you are seeking to influence think about the issue? Are they likely to listen to you? Are they vulnerable to pressure in some way? Do they have the power to actually get things done?
- How is your idea better? If there is an obvious problem and you can make the case that solving it will bring benefit, it will be easier to make progress

If you can think through the answers to these questions, you will:

- Be clear about what you want
- Know who to focus on to get what you want
- Have a strong argument supported by evidence
- Be able to deal confidently with any challenges to your campaign

3. Knowing What You Want

So, you've identified a focus for your campaign, you know what you want to change or what issue you want to raise awareness about, now you've got to stop dreaming and turn your ideas into action.

It might sound obvious, but if you're going to get it right from the start, you need to have a clear idea of exactly what the campaign is about and what you hope to achieve. In other words, what is your basic message; what do you want to change? This will be the aim of your campaign. No matter how good your strategy (plan of action) is, you won't get anywhere if your message doesn't work.

Having a clear message will help you to identify how you are going to communicate the purpose of your campaign to other people in order to enlist their support.

However big or small your campaign, you need to decide what's different about what you're doing and use it to your advantage, to help you stand out from other campaigners, and ultimately help you to achieve your goal.

This will help you to come up with your campaign rationale – a statement about why you are going to campaign on this particular issue.

Being clear about this will help you to communicate effectively with the public and media when they question you about your campaign and why they should take an interest in it.

Top Tip — Knowing What You Want

To help you come up with a clear, basic aim for your campaign, think about:

- What is it that you're asking for?
- What is the problem with the way things currently are?
- What's the solution as you see it?
- Why do you want it?

You might want to check out session plan 9 page 44

4. What's Your Campaign Message?

This is a short, snappy statement that will be your key communication tool with the public and media. It should be a simple message about your campaign issue that you want people to remember, and which will encapsulate why the issue is important and why people should care about it. It should be the way in which you engage people with your campaign.

Your message will be the "brand" for your campaign and it should tell people who you are, what you do and how you do it. It should help to mark you out as unique. Find your identity and stick to it!

It should sum up what you want people to think of when they think of you and your campaign. Thinking about what your campaign values are will help you to define your message.

The art of developing campaign messages and catchy slogans comes down to turning the main arguments for why someone should back your campaign into simple and meaningful language that will appeal to your key audience. Message is what separates one campaign from another and it drives your campaign strategy.

Examples of good slogans include:

Barack Obama:	Change we can believe in
Labour, 1997:	Because Britain Deserves Better
Tories:	Labour isn't working.
Heinz:	Beanz Meanz Heinz
Orange:	The Future's Bright, The Future's Orange
Hampshire UKYP:	WiFi: It's Where It's @

Developing a clear message can save you time (and money) as you are more likely to identify who you need to influence correctly and to convince those you do reach. It is therefore essential to devote time at the start of your campaign to analysing your own and your opponents' strengths and weaknesses, as well as what issues most concern people, and focusing your campaign on these issues.

Of course there will be times when you will be forced to react to things people who are opposed to your campaign are saying or doing, but as far as possible you should aim to develop two or three coherent reasons for people to support you, and stick to those messages throughout the campaign.

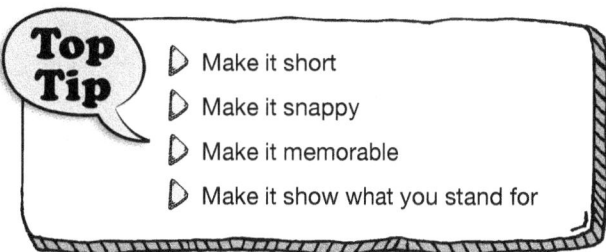

Top Tip
- Make it short
- Make it snappy
- Make it memorable
- Make it show what you stand for

5. Knowing Who to Influence

Next you're going to need to identify who you want / need to persuade if your campaign is to be successful. Every campaign needs at least one focal point.

These are the individual, group, corporation or statutory body that can actually create (or prevent) the change that your campaign is about. Having a clearly identified focal point and a specific set of messages, will give your campaign both clarity and impact.

So, identify who you should be working with and who you can get to support you. These people will be your focal points and you will need to aim your message at them.

What Makes Them Tick?

It can be useful to "map" the forces that will influence who you want to persuade.

You need to think about:
- What motivates them?
- What makes them happy?
- What influences them?
- Who influences them?
- Are they "friends" of your campaign, opponents, or not sure?
- How do you connect with them?

You might want to check out session plan 6 page 40

INFORMATION SHEETS

You might want to check out session plan 7 page 42

Find out who makes the decisions and at what levels. Is there more than one decision-maker that you need to focus on? If your campaign has more than one focal point, you may need to think about changing your message and objective (what you're hoping to achieve) to suit them. For example, if your campaign is about getting a local skate park:

- Focal point: The general public. Message: 'I want the public to sign our petition to get a skate park'
- Focal point: The local authority. Message: 'I want the council to provide the land and funding for the skate park'
- Focal point: A company. Message: 'I want Company X to offer to provide the equipment for the skate park'
- Focal point: Local young people. Message: 'I want you all to come to the proposed site of the skate park at a particular time for a photo opportunity'

Always make sure your campaign has a clear focal point. That way, when someone asks you who your campaign is focussing on and what you want them to do, you can give them a clear and simple answer and you'll be well on your way to getting your message out there.

6. Building Your Case

Once you've decided what it is you want to achieve, you need to start building your case, in order to help you convince other people.

Know Your Stuff

For your campaign to be successful, you are going to need to do some research, to get evidence to support the claims you are making about both the situation as it is today and how it could be better if certain changes were made. If you take note of the following guidelines when collecting your evidence, you'll be well on your way to building a strong and reliable case:

- Check thoroughly any information and facts you collect
- Make sure your sources are reliable
- If you can get an expert opinion to back up your case, use it
- Be truthful – don't be tempted to exaggerate details in support of your case
- Don't use only parts of research that support what you want to say and ignore the rest. It can always be used against you to help discredit your campaign
- Keep your evidence focussed – stick to your main issue. Chances are the people you're trying to influence won't have much time to look at it and yours won't be the only campaign they're being asked to consider.
- Try where possible to link your evidence to fit in with the priorities of whoever you're trying to influence
- Propose a solution – offering a realistic alternative is much better than just moaning about what's wrong with the way things are
- Try and find out if there have been similar campaigns before and what the solutions were then. What are the risks of not listening to what you are proposing?
- People's real-life experiences of an issue can make for both powerful and persuasive evidence. Throw in some well-researched facts and this can provide a winning combination

Find out how the people you are seeking to influence prefer to receive information and try and present your evidence to suit that

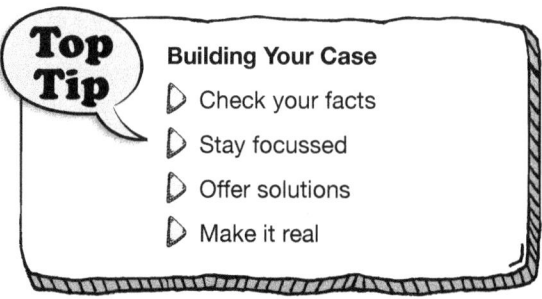

Top Tip

Building Your Case
- Check your facts
- Stay focussed
- Offer solutions
- Make it real

You might want to check out session plan 12 page 46

7. Evidence Gathering

You can collect evidence to support your case from a variety of sources, depending on the issue. These include:

- The internet
- Newspaper articles
- Local or national statistics, from published figures and surveys
- Other groups who might be affected by the same issue that you could talk to, or who might have evidence you could use
- You could do a survey – that will help you find out the opinions of other people and may prove useful later on in the campaign, when you're looking to demonstrate success
- Anecdotal information – your own experience or case studies and stories from like-minded people or people in a similar situation are also worth collecting
- Visual evidence – photographs or video (e.g. if you want to improve the condition of a playground etc)
- Academic evidence – are there any research projects and reports you could make use of?

Remember that you will need to gather all the evidence you can find that will support your case, but also any evidence that might be used against you. This will help you to be prepared to deal with any opposition you might come up against.

If you're looking for reports, statistics and general background information, good starting points for gathering evidence include:

- Newspapers / their websites
- BBC website
- Local Council website
- Government department / agency websites
- Relevant charity and pressure group websites
- Parliament website, including Hansard
- www.theyworkforyou.com – good way to lobby your MP
- Office for National Statistics
- Your local library
- Community groups / tenants' associations
- Google

You might want to check out session plan 13 page 48

8. Planning Your Campaign

Knowing what you want to do, how you'll do it, who will do it and by when will get you off to a strong start. By the time you get to the stage of planning your campaign in more detail, you should already:

- Have come up with a clear aim
- Know who to focus on to get what you want
- Have come up with a short, snappy campaign message
- Have a strong argument supported by evidence

Next step then, will be to identify the smaller steps you want to take in order to achieve your campaign aim. These steps are your campaign objectives.

Setting SMART Objectives

You should try to make each of your objectives SMART – specific, measurable, achievable, realistic and within a timescale.

- Specific, so that each step you identify has a clear purpose
- Measurable to help you gauge the progress you are making
- Achievable – the smaller, specific steps you choose will help to make the overall aim of your campaign feel more achievable
- Realistic – being realistic about what you can hope to achieve within a specific period of time will help you keep your campaign focussed
- Timescale – identify dates by when specific actions need to be taken

Once you've set your objectives, make sure you review them regularly, to make sure that they are still the most appropriate ones for you as your campaign progresses.

Information Sheets

INFORMATION SHEETS

Campaign Stages

▷ Next, you need to look at your objectives, what they involve and what timescales you have set for them, and then divide your campaign into different stages

▷ Often, your objectives will follow-on from each other in a logical sequence so it will be quite clear in what order you should do things.

▷ But if not, look at what are the simple, easy things to do, start with those and build-up from there

Campaign Tasks

▷ For each campaign stage, take the objective or part of the objective you are going to be working on, and break it down into the tasks you will need to do to achieve that. This will include things like doing research, contacting your MP, designing a leaflet or survey etc

▷ The tasks should be as specific as possible, and should include details of how they are going to be done

9. Coming Up With An Action Plan

Having worked out what the first stage of your campaign is going to be, and the key tasks that form part of that stage, you then need to put this information into an action plan.

> **Top Tip**
>
> **Action Planning**
>
> ▷ Set out the objective (or part of the objective) you are going to be working on, with the different tasks listed underneath
>
> ▷ Then work out who is going to carry out each task, and agree when they will do that
>
> ▷ Remember to include a column in your table for monitoring the progress made, so you are clear about how you are going to check that you are on track
>
> ▷ The best way of doing this is probably to set aside 5-10 minutes at each meeting for reviewing where you have got up to and whether the tasks have been met

Reviewing and Strengthening Your Campaign

▷ There will always be a chance that things will not go quite as you first planned. Try to be prepared with some clear ideas of what scenarios could occur, and how you would respond to these

▷ Carry out a SWOT exercise – an analysis of the strengths, weaknesses, opportunities and threats of your campaign

▷ Strengths and weaknesses are the things that are in your control, they are the strengths and weaknesses of your group / organisations. Opportunities and threats come from outside

▷ For strengths, think about what your advantage is – what are you contributing that others are not?

▷ Identify where you are stronger and more able than anyone else campaigning on the issue.

▷ For weaknesses, is there anything that may be harmful to the campaign?

▷ Think about resources, how much can you, your group / organisation take on?

▷ Opportunities: are there dates coming up which you could take advantage of?

▷ Is there a celebrity who may be interested in the campaign?

▷ What outside aspects / opportunities are there which could be helpful in achieving your objectives?

▷ Threats: are there any outside aspects that could be harmful to achieving your objectives?

▷ Is there anyone that may stand in your way?

You might want to check out session plan 14 page 49

Case Study

Lesbian and Gay Youth Manchester

Lesbian and Gay Youth Manchester (LGYM) is a Lesbian, Gay, Bisexual and Trans (LGBT) project for LGBT's aged 14 to 25.

The project provides a safe space for LGBT young people and runs a variety of activities, including training residentials, outdoor activities, film making and drama.

The group has produced a number of DVDs, which they use as part of workshops they deliver to other young people. For example, they made a DVD about conflict resolution for primary school children, with the aim of trying to teach people of a younger age that conflicts are the same whether it's an argument between two people or you're having a war.

The group is also campaigning to stop sexist and homophobic language in everyday life, e.g. "that phone is so gay". One of the ways in which they do this is through work in schools to educate people. Young people from the project go into schools and run workshops over a period of 3 weeks, with the aim of challenging stereotypes about LGBT people. They are now going to start targeting school councils and prefects, offering training on equality and diversity as a way of challenging homophobia, and are looking to develop their links with the National Union of Teachers to roll their programme out.

What young people from Lesbian and Gay Youth Manchester say about campaigning…

- Young people have the right to freedom of speech too
- We should be allowed to have our say
- Youth is a part of the community too
- It's important we have a say now, because we are the ones who will have to live with the consequences of the decisions made by the older generation
- You've got to try and change people's mind set – make them realise that just because the issue hasn't affected them personally, it's still important
- Think of ways you can try and change their mind set – look at how motivational speakers manage to convince people to change their minds
- You've got to make an emotional connection with the audience in some way – if you can convince them that something is happening or could happen, they are more likely to be swayed round to your point of view because there's more of a chance they'll care
- Try not to divert off the point of your campaign
- Know your stuff – do your research about laws and the issue you're campaigning for
- Look at other parts of the world as well and see what they've done

Information Sheets

INFORMATION SHEETS

10. Building a Team

You might want to check out session plan 15 page 51

It's very difficult to run a campaign single-handedly, so you're going to need to build a team of people, who are committed to your cause – your campaign group.

A campaign group should help draw up the plan and make sure things get done. This can help you to establish who will take responsibility for which tasks and avoid the problem of too much work falling to too few people, who might then lose interest in the campaign very quickly.

Top Tip

Team Building

- Think about what skills it would be good to have within your campaign group – e.g. website design, fundraising, public speaking, artistic ability, knowledge of how the council works etc

- Everybody's got something to offer, so try and build a team who have a good mix of skills and will be able to perform the different roles needed as you progress

- Encourage people who want to be involved to think about what they are good at

- Try getting them to think of 5 things they are good it, to encourage everyone to recognise what their individual skills are

- If people get stuck, encourage people to describe other group members' strengths

- Remember that within the group, individuals are likely to want to assume different levels of responsibility, according to their existing skills, confidence and experience

- Some people will be happy just to take part in campaign activities, whilst others may want to plan and lead on them. For more information and ideas on the differing ways in which people can get involved in your campaign group, see the Campaign Challenges section of this toolkit

11. Evaluating Your Campaign

Evaluation is the way in which you measure the progress of your campaign and eventually what has been achieved as a result of it.

Why evaluate your campaign?

For starters, if you don't evaluate your campaign, how will you know if you've been successful? It's also a good way of identifying and learning from your mistakes.

Evaluation should be an on-going process, which is carried out on a regular basis throughout the campaign. Starting with clear aims and measurable objectives will make this process easier, as it means you can keep on reviewing how far they have been met. Key points / successes / set backs should be recorded as they happen, to help you to learn from them.

Start as you mean to go on

From the beginning of your campaign you need to be thinking about what success would look like. What changes will be made that enable you to say you've been successful and who will they affect?

Are they:

- Changes which will have an effect on the lives of children and young people?
- Changes in a particular policy or practice?
- Changes in the wider community?

It might be that the changes you are looking for as part of your campaign cover several of these areas – e.g. you're campaigning for the voting age to be reduced to 16. This requires a change of policy and will have an effect on the lives of young people.

Measuring Success

From the start of your campaign, you will need to think about what information you can collect and at what points (start, middle, end) to help you evaluate your progress. Collecting this information will help you to:

- Ensure your campaign is meeting its objectives, agreed timetables and deadlines
- Assess reasons for success and failure, and make changes where necessary
- Identify any possible gaps and opportunities
- Measure the success or otherwise of your campaign
- Identify the progress being made by the individuals involved in the campaign
- Identify opportunities for skills and knowledge development

12. How to Evaluate Your Campaign

There are a number of ways in which you can evaluate your campaign.

Qualitative methods: these will help you find out about people's perceptions of your campaign. Methods you could use include surveys, focus groups and one-to-one interviews. The effect is best assessed by the people your campaign was trying to help, so think carefully about how you involve them in your evaluation.

Quantitative methods: these help you to cross-check people's perceptions with other sources of data in order to obtain objective information. It might involve collecting information about the number of people involved in the campaign, or using other sets of regular and relevant statistics.

Some key questions to ask as part of your evaluation:

- Is the campaign achieving its aims?
- If not, why is that?
- Are you getting the reaction you wanted?
- Are you getting the result you wanted?
- If so, is that result having the effect you were hoping for?
- Are there any effects of the campaign that you weren't expecting?
- What was good about your campaign?
- How did the young people involved benefit?
- What skills / knowledge do they have now that they didn't before?
- Is there anything you would do differently / better next time?
- What was the media reaction?
- What next?

Evaluation Checklist

- Use evidence. This can be existing data, like national statistics, previous reviews and evaluations, the record of a discussion or video footage, or a journal kept by a young person to document their own progress throughout the campaign. Without evidence, you are just making a subjective judgement
- Avoid sweeping statements, unless you can back them up with examples of evidence (e.g. a case study, a relevant statistic or both)
- Use different methods to investigate a particular issue
- Use quotes to back up what you're saying
- Respect anonymity where necessary
- Make sure you inform people who took part in / were interested in your campaign what the outcomes were. Make sure you give a summary to fellow campaigners and anyone else who helped you. This will help keep your supporters interested

Record and accredit the progress and achievements of the individuals involved

INFORMATION SHEETS

A. Campaign Checklist

It's important to remember that planning your campaign and actually "doing" your campaign are very much linked and shouldn't be treated as two separate activities. Using this checklist should help you make the connections between the two.

- What we want…
- Our campaign message is…
- Arguments for our campaign…
- Arguments against our campaign…
- Research methods we can use…
- Who we want to influence…
- How we will influence them…
- Our campaign objectives are…
- Our main campaign tasks are…

B. Campaigning Action Tools

So, you've got your campaign aim and you've set your objectives, you've come up with a catchy slogan, identified who you're going to need to persuade, and you've got a cunning a plan of action. Now, you've got to get on out there and start actually doing it.

What tactics / methods you want to use will vary according to your particular campaign.

You will need to try and find out where those you are seeking to influence stand on the issue you are campaigning on. That will help you to make sure the tactics and message you use are suitable. For example, how you present your campaign to a local councillor or MP will be different from how you present it to members of your local youth club.

Think about how you can get your message across to the key decision-makers (Councillors, MPs, School Governing Board etc). Sometimes you might be able to speak to them directly, but it's also quite likely you will have to go through other people (council officers, council committees, civil servants, special advisors etc). Try and think creatively about how to access these people – do you have personal contacts; can you use Trustees, other organisations or shared interest groups?

Different methods you could use include:

Posters

Good for:

- Advertising an event / speaker
- Using at a key stage in your campaign – e.g. if there's a vote about to take place
- Campaigns about a local issue – e.g. closure of a youth club / community centre

Things to watch out for:

- Not interactive
- Need to make them simple, bold, informative, direct
- Remember to include an address where people can find out more

Skills you will develop:

- Design
- Drawing
- Working on a computer
- Leaflets

Good for:

- Initial engagement
- Building a database of supporters
- Creating awareness in the street
- Basic information about your campaign / key messages
- Pointing people to sources of further information

Things to watch out for:

- Not interactive
- Need to make them simple, bold, informative, direct
- Need to have a snappy tag line
- Include a website address where people can find out more

Skills you will develop:

- Design
- Drawing
- Working on a computer
- Writing

Postcards

Good for:

- Getting mass sign up to your campaign
- Creating awareness of what you're trying to achieve
- Photo opportunities with the press

Things to watch out for:

- Need to make sure they are being used once they are distributed
- If you are targeting an individual, you can time the posting of the cards, so that something arrives in their post bag everyday, constantly reminding them of your issue

Skills you will develop:

- Design
- Working on a computer

INFORMATION SHEETS

Filming / vox pops

Good for:

- Being interactive
- Human interest – people like to hear what other people have to say about an issue
- Makes the issue seem more real / immediate – that's why newspapers / local TV like to use this method

Things to watch out for:

- Need to do something to make your piece stand out
- Make sure you ask the right questions to get good, interesting answers

Skills you will develop:

- Working with a video camera
- Interviewing skills
- Editing skills

Stalls at conferences / events

Good for:

- Presenting your message to a captive audience
- Could help to inspire people to get involved
- High visibility if done correctly

Things to watch out for:

- Problem is it's a bit one way
- Have to use this in conjunction with other methods
- You need a gimmick to get people's attention in the first place to get them on to the stall
- Then you need to make sure you get them to sign up / you get their details

Skills you will develop:

- Talking to other people
- Being creative
- Imagination

Demonstrations / protests

Good for:

- Getting media attention
- Can be a good way of getting lots of people involved in your campaign
- Can be a good method for raising general awareness of what you want

Things to watch out for:

- Demonstrations and protests are only effective if you have built up enough public support
- You need to have run a series of activities which build up to a demonstration if it's to be successful
- For example, if you want to build a campaign against climate change, you can't just set up a facebook group and invite people to a demonstration, you will need to get support from organisations and groups with a large activist base (such as Trade Unions, Friends of the Earth etc)

Skills you will develop:

- Being good at organising
- Imagination
- Being creative

Stunts

Good for:

- Getting your message across in an unusual and humorous way

Things to watch out for:

- Needs to be delivered with a purpose and in the right situation
- Stunts work well if they are backed up by extensive factual research and investigation

Skills you will develop:

- Imagination
- Being creative

Articles in newspapers / magazines

Good for:

- Creating wider community awareness
- Following up on a story to create continuity
- Photo opportunities
- Getting good quotes / third party endorsement (important because it shows wider support for your issue)

Things to watch out for:

- Make sure you include a human interest element / some quotes
- Back up your story with some key facts
- Once you contact a journalist, it's up to them how and when they use the information
- You may not be in control of the story

Skills you will develop:

- Writing
- Research
- Working on the computer

Surveys

Good for:

- Raising awareness of your campaign
- Demonstrating support for your campaign
- If done effectively, they can produce a juicy headline-grabbing statistic

Things to watch out for:

- Needs to be used in conjunction with other methods
- You need to be clear about what it is you're trying to find out
- Try using Survey Monkey: http://www.surveymonkey.com/ to design your survey
- You could use Zoho Polls: http://zohopolls.com/ to create online polls and embed them on your website

Skills you will develop:

- Writing
- Interview skills
- Research skills
- Working on a computer

Petitions / e-petitions

Good for:

- Building massive support
- It requires low-level commitment
- Good way to help build awareness of what you're asking for

Things to watch out for:

- As it only requires a minimum amount of commitment to sign up , it can be hard to build active support just using this method

Skills you will develop:

- Working on a computer

INFORMATION SHEETS

Songs and poems

Good for:

- Can be something catchy that sticks in people's minds
- Way to introduce humour – helps get extra publicity
- Ability to use it more than once

Things to watch out for:

- Bit one-way
- Don't want it to be dismissed as a gimmick

Skills you will develop:

- Being creative
- Singing
- Imagination

Drama

Good for:

- Raising awareness of an issue
- Acting out a potentially controversial situation in a safe way – especially where there's a tendency for people to take sides (e.g. a drama group in Northern Ireland used this to address issues of sectarianism)
- Using with school, college, youth and community groups

Things to watch out for:

- Time intensive
- Bit one-way

Skills you will develop:

- Performance skills
- Imagination
- Being creative

Facebook

Good for:

- Building mass support and interactivity
- Two-way communication – ask people to do something specific and get them to report back to you
- Good visual element – photos / post letters etc
- Good for signposting people to other ways to get involved with the campaign

Things to watch out for:

- Need to keep your page up-to-date and relevant
- Requires low level commitment

Skills you will develop:

- Working on a computer
- Design skills

Twitter

Good for:

- Promoting a single message
- Can help you build up a group of followers
- Can use it to challenge politicians directly (some politicians have days where they will take questions directly via Twitter)
- It's a good way to get an answer on the record from the people who make the decisions
- Create an account at Twitter: http://twitter.com/

Things to watch out for:

▷ Requires low-level commitment

▷ Can use it to reach supporters with a timely and relevant message at key points in your campaign

Skills you will develop:

▷ Working on a computer

Websites / Blogs

Good for:

▷ Signposting people to a single place for lots of information about your campaign

▷ Can help you to build up a group of followers

▷ Can use it to put up photos / video footage of your campaign

▷ Can put up templates of letters / petitions etc for people to use as part of your campaign

Things to watch out for:

▷ Need to make sure you keep your website up to date and relevant

▷ Requires low-level commitment

Skills you will develop:

▷ Working on a computer

▷ Website design

▷ Writing skills

Public meetings

Good for:

▷ Educating more people about the issue

▷ Finding potential activists

▷ Inviting politicians along to take part

▷ Good step for getting commitment for an action – and it will be a matter of public record

▷ Getting media / publicity for your campaign

Things to watch out for:

▷ Need a skilled chair

▷ Need to make sure commitments made at the meeting are followed up

▷ Make sure you hold them at a well-timed point in your campaign (e.g. leading up to a significant event, to help you build support)

Skills you will develop:

▷ Organisation skills

▷ Chairing skills

▷ Speaking in front of other people

School /college / university presentations

Good for:

▷ Presenting your message to a captive audience

▷ Could help to inspire people to get involved

Things to watch out for:

▷ It's a bit one way / not that interactive

▷ Need to use presentations in conjunction with other methods

Skills you will develop:

▷ Speaking in front of other people

INFORMATION SHEETS

> You might want to check out session plan 14 page 49

C. Raising Awareness

Changing the world – or even just a tiny part of it – means you're going to need support to make it happen. So here are some top tips for getting people on your side and building up that all-important bunch of loyal supporters:

- Publicise what you're up to and let people know how they can get in touch with you
- Build up a list of people who are keen to help out with all kinds of things, like putting up posters, delivering leaflets, organising protests etc
- Always make sure you give contact details when you're promoting your campaign or no one will be able to get in touch if they want to lend a hand
- Once they have got in touch, make sure you give them something to do or they'll lose interest
- Make sure you keep your supporters in touch with what's going on in the campaign on a regular basis and continue to let them know how they can help out
- Avoid the temptation to e-mail them every day and risk clogging up their in-boxes
- If you have a website or a facebook page, always make sure you answer questions and comments, so that people know you are listening
- Make suggestions on your website / facebook page about how people can get involved – e.g. by participating in a survey, putting a link to an online petition etc
- Set up a fan page for your campaign on facebook and put lots of interesting content on it (video clips, stories, articles etc)
- Check out what other related groups there are out there on social networking sites and make contact with the organisers

> You might want to check out session plan 18 page 54

D. Some Do's and Don'ts of Campaigning

- Don't be over-ambitious
- Do avoid getting overwhelmed by the issue
- Do match your aspirations to your resources
- Don't just jump on a bandwagon – campaign on something that's relevant to YOU
- Do make sure your evidence stands up to scrutiny
- Do be prepared
- Don't just preach to the converted
- Do be specific about who you are trying to influence and clear about why you have chosen them
- Don't just focus on the "general public" – the public is made up of diverse groups of people and individuals with different interests and motivations
- Do keep focussed
- Do be clear about how change will be achieved
- Do make sure it actually adds something to your campaign if you're going to join forces with other organisations to form an alliance
- Don't get out too soon – getting a policy changed is a success, but you may still want to see how the new one works out

Top Tip

UK Youth Voice
- "Campaigning is about fighting for your cause"
- "Stick with it"
- "Never give up"
- "Remember, you do have a voice"
- "If you don't succeed at first, persevere"
- "Aim high!"
- "No matter who you are, you have something to offer"

Case Study

Jeans for Genes

Jeans for Genes is a national campaign which raises money to change the world for children with genetic disorders.

Its main fundraising event is Jeans for Genes Day which takes place annually on the first Friday of October. Hundreds of thousands of people across the UK – and beyond – make a donation to wear their jeans to work or school. The money they raise helps to fund the care that children need now and the research that could change their lives in the future.

Working with Celebrity Endorsements

The charity was founded in the 1990s and has a long and successful history of working with celebrities to raise their profile. Examples of how they have done this include:

- Body painting Robbie Williams with spray on jeans – an image which was used across the press
- Using Jaime Winstone and Zoe Ball to promote the charity's merchandise and get £500,000 of free advertising in the media
- Developing an ongoing relationship with the children's TV character, Fifi and the Flowertots. Fifi does lots of personal appearances for the charity which means that children get to meet her and learn more about genetic disorders

Top Tip from Jeans for Genes

If you can, try and make use of personal connections. If you're lucky, it could be that someone within your group has a link to a celebrity, but chances are it's more likely to be about targeting a celebrity with a link to your cause.

Jeans for Genes managed to get Coleen Rooney to host the charity's 10th birthday party at Great Ormond Street. Coleen's sister has Rhett syndrome and it was her personal connection to the cause that led her to get involved with the charity.

Information Sheets

INFORMATION SHEETS

E. Get Lobbying

If you want to achieve change, you're going to need to influence those people with the power to make that change. This is also known as lobbying and it basically means putting pressure on or exercising influence over decision-makers in order to achieve your campaign aim.

Lobbying isn't something that has to be left to the experts: it's very simple and anyone with reasonably good manners can do it.

If you've done your homework, you'll be clear about who you are trying to influence – the right people or organisations to approach about your campaign. It could be your local councillor, head teacher, your MP, the local Mayor, a government minister, a Member of the European Parliament or perhaps a business corporation.

Once you've decided on who you need to lobby, that will help you to choose how best to lobby them. For example, whilst it might be possible to arrange a meeting with your local councillor or Mayor, you're much less likely to be able to arrange a face-to-face meeting with a government minister.

Lobbying comes in lots of different forms. You can write to people, e-mail them, go to your local councillor's or MP's surgery and meet them in person, you can phone people or you could contact them via things such as Twitter and Facebook.

You might want to check out session plan 17 page 53

F. Get Writing

You might want to check out session plan 17 page 53

It is quite likely that a lot of the people you are trying to influence (politicians, companies etc) tend to receive a large number of letters every week, so you need to think about how to make your letter stand out. Try:

- **Keeping it short.** A one-sided typed letter with clear headings will help make sure they read all the information

- **Stick to one issue per letter.** Even if you have a number of things you want to raise, it's better to write a different letter for each one. This way any of the more difficult issues won't get "lost" in the middle of the others

- **Make it local.** Grab their attention by letting them know what's happening in the area that they are elected to represent / they operate in. Tell them that that is where you live

- **Give examples.** Use the evidence and statistics you found to show how many people are affected by this issue

- **Make it personal.** Politicians will generally respond to individual letters, but not to standard letters. So if you're asking lots of people to contact a politician about a specific issue, ask them to make their letters slightly different. If you've met the politician before, always refer to the last time you met or contacted them. Always include your contact details

- **Give them an action.** Be clear about what you want and how they can help you achieve it

- **Keep in regular contact.** If your issue isn't going to be resolved quickly, then let them know you're serious by sending updates to support your argument, such as press cuttings, or extracts of new evidence. The more informed they are, the better able they will be to influence debates at both the local and national level

G. Face to Face Meetings

Meeting those you are hoping to influence (councillors, MPs, other decision makers etc) is often the best way to ask them to help you to take action e.g. in the local council or Parliament.

Getting the most out of your meeting

If you don't know where the person stands on your issue before you go in, then don't expect immediate commitment to your campaign. They may well want to go away and find out more but here are some tips to help you get the most out of your meeting:

Do...

- Prepare a short typed brief – two sides of A4 maximum, with key points and essential statistics
- Take notes
- Offer to follow up with more information
- Watch the time and ensure you give them an opportunity to respond
- Consider inviting them to the site if your case can be better made visually (e.g. if you're asking them to back your fight for improvements to something in your community)
- Ask them what they can and will do
- Follow-up with a short thank you letter and summary of your key points

Don't...

- Use jargon or abbreviations
- Quote hundreds of percentages or statistics
- Assume that they already have prior knowledge of your issue
- Overstate your case
- Verbally attack or be over-critical of them or the political party they represent
- Feel you need to know all the answers
- Lose hope if they don't agree with you straightaway

You might want to check out session plan 21 page 62

H. Shout About It!

You might want to check out session plan 18 page 54

Dealing with the Media

At some stage during your campaign, you're going to need to involve the media, to help generate extra publicity and interest in what you're trying to achieve.

When looking to involve the media, it's important to remember that, even though journalists might seem a bit frightening and out of your reach, they actually need you. Without people like you getting in touch and telling them interesting stories they would have nothing to write about. Journalism is supposed to be all about finding those stories, but sometimes it's worth giving journalists a bit of a helping hand by putting yourself right in front of their noses.

There are three main things you do

1. Work out what you want to say
2. Work out who you need to say it to
3. Get in touch and say it

You can involve the media in two ways:

- By writing to the letters page of a newspaper
- By contacting a journalist directly with a story

Writing to the letters page of a newspaper

The letters page is one of the most read pages of any newspaper. To increase your chances of getting your letter published, try and pick a newspaper that is likely to be sympathetic to your point of view. However, if there's a newspaper which publishes an article that's anti-your campaign or that concerns you, then you could also consider this as an invitation to comment.

Increase your chances of getting published by:

- Sending your letter in the same day that the article is published and by the deadline set
- Refer to the article on which you're commenting and the date it was published
- Be clear whether you are providing facts or opinion
- Keep it short and to the point (aim for between 45 and 200 words)
- Include your name and relevant contact details in case the editor needs to check facts

Information Sheets

INFORMATION SHEETS

Right Track

Right Track is a drop-in centre that works with Black and Minority Ethnic young people in the justice system in Bristol.

A group of young people from Right Track had the opportunity to make a DVD on a topic of their choosing. They decided to make it about racism.

The film, called Listen Here, took 6 weeks to make and featured the group acting out various incidents, to help people understand more about the issues being discussed. The film has been shown to the police, Bristol Youth Offending Team and local youth workers. It has also been used in presentations and shown in schools around the area. It is now being used as a training tool for professionals, to give them an insight into young people's experiences of racism.

Having finished that film, the group then went on to make another one on the subject of Stop and Search with the BBC.

What young people from Right Track say about campaigning…

- Online petitions are easier than paper ones, as it's easier to send them to people and get lots of responses from local people and people that live further away
- Councillors are good people to go to, as they can have influence and it helps you to build a bridge between young people and adults
- You have to go straight to people, rather than expecting them to come to you
- Design a website that people can access at school
- Make your website young people friendly – put DVDs / vox pops on it
- Get other young people to help you set up your site – like a group of volunteers. This will make them feel part of your campaign
- It's good if people can get something out of their involvement – you could maybe use incentives
- You have to get people to realise what the benefits are to them
- Run groups to get people involved in different ways
- Plays are a very good way of making a point and getting a message across – people can learn from them. They can relate to a character in a play and it makes a more interesting way to get a point across

I. Contacting Journalists

Try contacting a journalist directly with a story, rather than waiting for them to come to you. Journalists tend to be busy people under great time pressure, who will usually be working on more than one story at a time. So, before you even think about picking up the phone to contact them, think about the following:

▷ How are you going to make them care about what you have to say?

▷ Do you have a story to tell? People like to hear about other people, so stories with an element of "human interest", for example case studies and quotes, are always more attractive than just straight facts.

▷ Can you support it with facts and figures? In other words, do you sound convincing?

▷ Are you willing to "go public" and be quoted?

▷ Are their readers / audience likely to share your view?

Local media

▷ People tend to be more trusting of local media / papers and radio

▷ If you can build up a good relationship with a local journalist, by spending time with them and talking to them, it will pay dividends

▷ Can you offer to do a young people's column?

Remember that journalists are always looking for a story. However, once you've given them one, you can't change your mind and it's up to them how and when they use the information. Sometimes the story can end up being very different from how you imagined!

You might want to check out session plan 18 page 54

J. Writing Press Releases

You might want to check out session plan 18 page 54

Basically, a press release is something which is written and its news. It can be sent out to papers, magazines, radio and TV stations. Journalists receive them all the time, so whilst it might be important to you and your campaign, it's nothing special to them.

Top Tips for Writing a Press Release

▷ Keep it short, sharp and to the point

▷ Be ruthless – make sure that everything that's in it really needs to be there and is telling an important part of your story

▷ Think tabloid – eye-catching quotes and headlines

▷ Know your audience

▷ Think about whether you're writing it for a paper, the TV or radio

▷ Don't include any attachments

▷ Include the date

▷ Include a headline

▷ Tell them WHO is doing it

▷ Tell them WHAT is happening

▷ Tell them WHERE it is happening

▷ Tell them WHEN it is happening

▷ Tell them WHY it is happening

▷ Include a note to the editor at the end, with information on who to phone for interviews or photos, and a brief bit of any relevant background information on the organisation / campaign

Information Sheets

INFORMATION SHEETS

K. Working with Third Party Endorsements

Celebrity endorsement

Getting a 'celebrity' to back your campaign could give it that extra boost that helps to get other people involved or shows people that you mean business. Think about all of the different causes that different celebrities back; sometimes they get paid, but if it is something they care about they will often do it for free.

Don't be intimidated by the challenge – getting a celebrity to back your campaign does not mean that they have to come on a demonstration with you! It could be something as simple as getting them to agree to let you use their picture or give a quick quote saying why they support your cause.

The best place to start is to do a bit of research – who do you want and why do you think they might be interested in being involved? Once you've got someone in mind, find their contact details (this will probably be an agent who represents them). Think very carefully about your approach – they are busy people and if your letter/email/call doesn't grab their attention from the start, you might find it difficult!

Things to remember:

- You need a long lead-in time – people can underestimate how much time it takes to get someone on board and you have to go through their agents who can be very difficult

- You have to have a very clear idea of what you want, but be willing to negotiate

- People have an unrealistic idea of engaging with celebrities – be realistic – accept they are very busy people

- Manage your expectations of who you might be able to get – it doesn't have to be the most famous person in the world, they just have to be relevant to you

- Ask for something simple – it might be as basic as getting them to sign off on a quote for you

- Who do you know who knows someone? Can you go down a back-door route to access them? What about a celebrity that used to go to your school?

- What is in it for them? Maybe you are offering them the chance to be associated with a good cause that might make them look good!

L. Public Speaking

You might want to check out session plan 20 page 60

The important thing to remember about public speaking is that actually, anyone can do it. And that includes you. In fact, you've probably done a bit of it before, even if you didn't call it that (talking to your youth group, your class etc).

Here, we offer you a few tips to help you get the most out of the experience.

- Confidence – that's the most important thing. If you believe in what you are saying and feel comfortable about your message you're already almost there!
- You may still get nervous, but turn that to your advantage and use it as a way to keep you focussed on what you've got to say
- Concentrate on your breathing – focus on one breath at a time
- Think about your feet – where are they? (Sounds weird, but it works!)
- Remember that the audience want you to succeed
- Remind yourself that you are the world expert on this little topic!
- Eye contact – make and maintain eye contact as it helps to come across more confidently. Remember not to stare but to look away or around the room every so often
- Stick to time – it is important not to overrun. If you are given ten minutes, try and make sure you don't go over that time – practising your talk will help
- Adopt the right facial expression – adopting an expression to suit what you're saying reinforces your presentation
- Watch your tone, pitch and volume – lower your tone to sound more convincing and don't speak too quickly. Speaking too loudly makes you sound aggressive, but speaking too quietly makes you appear unsure of what you are saying
- Watch your hand signals – be aware of what you are doing, a wagging finger can seem aggressive; (excessive) movement of the hand may express nervousness
- Stand straight, walk tall – having hunched shoulders and a slouched posture can give the impression that you are nervous and unsure of yourself and what you are saying
- Look good to feel good – find a style that makes you look and feel good. Also think about the clothes you will be wearing, as it is important to dress appropriately
- Turn off your phone! There is nothing worse than your phone ringing when you're giving a talk. Not only does it give a bad impression, it can also affect your confidence

Information Sheets

INFORMATION SHEETS

M. Planning a Presentation

Good preparation is the key to an effective presentation or speech. The more you know about what you want to say and who you are saying it to, the easier it is to write.

- Find out who your audience is. What sort of language do they use?
- Find out where you will be speaking. Will it be from a lectern, table in a large room, standing up or sitting down?
- How many people will be listening to your presentation? Will you know any of them personally?
- How long is your presentation? The general rule is to keep it short and sweet
- Be creative with your time, using visual aids (video, overheads) to break it up
- Is it just you giving the presentation or is there a group of you?
- If there's a group of you, is everybody clear about what their role is and when they have to do their bit?
- Make sure you've got a prompt, to help you remember what you want to say. You could write your speech out or at least prepare some notes. Postcards or bullet points on small sheets of paper are better than long sheets of text
- If possible practice in the room where you will be giving your presentation

Structuring your presentation

A well structured presentation starts by telling the audience what you're going to say, goes on to explain the details, and ends with a summary of the key points you want the audience to remember.

- Keep things in threes, it focuses attention and is easier to remember what you said
- Beginning – introduce yourself / the others you are presenting with and what you'll be speaking about
- Middle – focus on three key aspects/ themes related to the subject you are speaking on
- End – summarise what you've said, including a closing remark or thought

You might want to check out session plan 21 page 62

N. Negotiation Skills

You might want to check out session plan 18 page 54

Effective negotiation helps you to resolve situations where what you want conflicts with what someone else wants.

Chances are that at some point during your campaign, you're going to need to do some negotiating to help you achieve your aim. Depending on the situation you are in, you will need to use different types of negotiation.

If you only need to deal with the person or group once – e.g. if you were in Dragon's Den asking for money to fund your latest invention – you will try to get as much as you can from the people you're negotiating with. However, if you're going to need to stay on good terms with the people you are negotiating with, so that you can work together in the future – e.g. you are negotiating with the local Residents' Association to get a local youth shelter – then it will be more important to make sure that everyone goes away from the negotiations feeling that they have got at least some of what they wanted.

Anyway, here you'll find some useful pointers to get you started:

Preparing for a successful negotiation...

- Set your **objective** – identify what it is you want to achieve
- Identify the other person's **'expected outcomes'** – find out what it is they want to get, and how far they might be prepared to compromise
- Work out the type of **relationships** between different people in the room. Are there any factors which might make a difference to how people work together?
- Consider the **consequences** – what would happen if you get what you want? What would happen to the other person?
- Where is the **power** in the negotiation? Who controls the resources? Who can influence others?
- Decide what you will **trade** – know what you are willing to give up or compromise as well as what you are unwilling to give up.
- Think about **alternatives** to your initial solution which could also get the result you want.
- Identify some **possible solutions**

ukyouth Hearing Unheard Voices

O. Making Meetings Work

Meetings are going to be an essential part of your campaign, so how can you go about making sure you get the most out of them?

All meetings involve a combination of speaking to a group, listening, negotiation and decision making. Meetings are much more effective if you follow some simple rules:

- Clear aim: what do you want to have decided by the end of the meeting?
- Preparation: what do you need to know in order to contribute effectively?
- Defined roles: who are the people at the meeting speaking for?

The aim of all meetings is the same – to come to a decision as a group.

Roles in a meeting

All formal meetings have a chair and a secretary, and some bigger meetings will also have a vice-chair. In some groups these roles can rotate, and in others they are always the same people.

- Chair: makes sure that the meeting runs smoothly, that everyone has their say and that a decision is made by the end of the meeting. This does not necessarily mean that they have the most power to make decisions – it just means that they are in charge of making sure the rest of the group can work together
- Vice-chair: in bigger meetings, the vice-chair's role is to support the chair, for example if they are unable to attend the meeting or if the group is split to make a decision
- Secretary: they are in charge of organising meetings and making sure that the right people are invited. They are also responsible for preparing the agenda and the minutes of the meeting

Keep a Record

It is important to keep a record of your meetings. This is partly to ensure that they run smoothly, and partly to make sure that people who were not at the meeting can find out what happened. It is also a good way of holding people to account when they have promised to do something.

Meetings usually have an agenda, which is distributed either before the meeting by post or email or at the start, and lists the topics that the meeting is going to discuss.

During the meeting someone (the secretary) will need to keep a record of who was at the meeting and what decisions were made. This record is called the minutes, and can be used to remind people of what they promised to do!

Case Study

UK Youth Voice

UK Youth Voice (Voice) is a youth led organisation within UK Youth that is dedicated to giving 16-25 year olds a voice. Voice hosts an Annual Conference, which brings young people from throughout the UK together to discuss the issues relevant to their lives and futures. Each year, the conference participants vote on the top four issues – known as resolutions – that young people face and then work on them throughout the rest of the year.

Know Your Stuff

Young people attending the Voice conference voted on a resolution which highlighted their perception that there is a negative portrayal of young people in the media, with young people's voices not being heard.

Voice wanted to find out if other young people also felt this way and decided to conduct an online survey, to establish:

- If young people feel they are misrepresented in the media
- If the media is portraying a balanced view of young people from a young person's perspective
- Ways in which young people could challenge their image in the media themselves

Of the 588 young people who took part in the survey, 84% felt that the media has had a bad effect on the image of young people, with more negative stories about young people than positive ones. Young people were also asked for their ideas on how to create more positive media coverage of young people. The top 3 suggestions were:

- Get more involved in positive activities in the community
- Write articles for newspapers and magazines
- Run media training at youth clubs or school

Voice members are now using what they found out from this survey to help them plan and run their campaign on how to improve the image of young people in the media.

What Voice say about campaigning...

- Make the most of technology – it only takes one line on Twitter to change the world!
- Get involved – you'll get loads out of it!
- Make it fun, make it engaging – that way people will want to get involved and stay involved.
- Even changing the smallest thing can give you an amazing sense of achievement.
- Make sure you recognise all the small things you manage to achieve along the way.
- Getting involved in a campaign should be on your list of 100 things to do before you die!
- You can make a difference!

SAMPLE SESSION PLANS AND ACTIVITY SHEETS

This section contains a variety of session plans and activity sheets that link to some of the activities, challenges and targets listed in the toolkit.

They are intended as suggestions only and you should feel free to adapt the session plans and activities to best suit the needs of your group.

Contents

Session Plans
1. What is a Campaign?
2. Getting Your Voice Heard
3. Have Your Say
4. Defining the Issue
5. Choosing a Campaign Goal
6. Choosing Who To Focus On
7. Debating the Issue
8. Balloon Exercise
9. Deciding on your Message
10. What Makes a Good Slogan?
11. £5 note exercise
12. Steps to the Future
13. Planning a Campaign
14. Action Planning
15. Team building
16. What I Want to Achieve
17. Lobbying Exercises
18. Dealing with the Media
19. Negotiating and Influencing
20. Practicing Public Speaking
21. Running a Public Meeting
22. Setting up a Facebook Group or Page
23. Setting up a Twitter Feed
24. Starting a Blog
25. Creating an Online Survey

Activity Sheets
- 1A. What is a Campaign?
- 3A. Debating Topics
- 4A. Defining the Issue
- 6A. Influence Map
- 8A. Balloon Template
- 12A. Footprints Template
- 13A. Planning a Campaign Scenario
- 14A. Action Plan Pro-Forma
- 14B. SWOT Analysis
- 16A. What I Want to Achieve Pro-Forma
- 18A Selling In Exercise
- 18B Writing a Press Release
- 19A. Negotiating Skills Sheet
- 19B. How should the Council spend its money?
- 20A. Planning Your Presentation
- Evaluation Pro-Forma

SAMPLE SESSION PLANS AND ACTIVITY SHEETS

1. What is a campaign?

Aim: To enable young people to differentiate between an issue and a campaign.

Time: 35 minutes

What you need:
Prompt sheet
Pens
Paper

Plan:

Divide young people in to pairs and ask them to come up with a list of things they would like to see changed. It can range from something very small and local, through to national and global issues.

Then get the young people to discuss and note down what actions they currently take or could take to set about changing the things they don't like.

Come back into one group and go through what they have come up with.

Questions for discussion:

- Why have they chosen the actions they have?
- Are these one-off things that they will do or are they part of a wider set of actions they will take to try and get what they want?
- Is it something they do by themselves, or do they join up with other people / organisations?
- Who are they targeting with these actions?
- Why have they chosen those people?

(20 minutes)

Then ask the group if any of them has ever participated in a campaign. If anyone has, ask them to tell the group a bit more about it.

Now, in two columns marked "Campaign" and "Other Action" list the things that the group feel tend to make something a campaign or are features of a campaign, and those that are not. Do any of the actions they listed on the activity sheet constitute a campaign? Why? Use the prompt sheet to help young people with this part of the exercise.

The aim of this is to enable young people to differentiate between an issue and a campaign, so that they start to see that campaigns are not just about one-off actions, but are part of a series of activities which want to convince people of a particular cause or influence their decisions through the use of persuasion.

(15 minutes)

1A Prompt Sheet: What Is a Campaign?

- Sign a petition
- Join a Facebook group
- Go on a demonstration
- Organise a public meeting
- Write a blog
- Wear a wristband
- Wear a badge
- Write a letter to an MP
- Fill out a survey
- Join an organisation (like Friends of the Earth)
- Stand for election
- Write letter to a newspaper
- Posting something on Twitter

2. GETTING YOUR VOICE HEARD

Aim: To consider the importance of having a voice on issues of concern

Time: 20 minutes

What you need:
Coloured card – several different colours.

Plan:

Play a game where someone gets left out.

Either:

- Seat the group in a circle
- Give everyone in turn the name of a fruit; apple, orange, banana, pear
- Call a fruit and everyone of that name must change places
- While they are dashing about remove one chair or more, so that people are left at the side and can no longer play

Or:

Give the different colour cards to each participant – e.g. one third of the group gets a blue card, one third a red card and the rest a green card. Any one who has a red card is ignored by the facilitator in the discussion. Ask the group a question to provoke a debate, e.g. "should voting be compulsory?"

Go round the group and ignore the people with the red card. Do a second round and only listen to people with a green card etc.

- Who might the red cards represent? The green cards?
- Who gets left out in society?
- Who isn't listened to? Who is?

Choose one of these two activities, then at the end of the game, discuss:

- How did it feel to be ignored/left out?
- Who has the power in the game?

3. HAVE YOUR SAY!

Aim: To encourage young people to have their say about issues that matter to them.

Time: 20-30 minutes

What you need:
Debating topic sheet

Please note that the sheet contained here is just a suggestion. You could debate a topic chosen by the group or issues that are particularly relevant to them.

Plan:

Divide the group into two halves, to make the session easier to manage. The Chair of each group reads a statement from the list of debating topics. Then they lead the debate and get discussion going around the room. The debates will last no longer than 10 minutes. The debates should be facilitated so that everyone is encouraged to air their views.

3A. DEBATING TOPICS

- Public transport is a good resource...
- Football is better than rugby...
- Money is one of the most important things in life...
- Voting is a waste of time...
- Reality TV is a good thing in our society...
- Libraries don't need books anymore...
- Young people today are uncaring and insensitive...
- Dogs are better than cats
- Email is a better form of communication than writing letters...
- The age for taking a driving test should be 21...
- The media spend too much time chasing celebrities...
- Mobile phones are essential to daily life...
- Anger is not a useful emotion...
- There are too many adverts...
- The voting age should be lowered to 16...
- School uniform should be abolished...
- Sweet is better than savoury...

Sample Session Plans and Activity Sheets

SAMPLE SESSION PLANS AND ACTIVITY SHEETS

4. DEFINING THE ISSUE

Aim: To help young people decide on their campaign issue and assess whether it's the right issue for them.

Time: 1 hour 20 minutes

What You Need:
Prompt sheet
Pens
Paper
Cards
Flipchart paper

Plan:

Ask the group to quick think all the issues that they would like to do something about / raise awareness of. Write up as a list on the flipchart paper. Is it something that they want to change, something they want to stop happening, or an issue they want to raise awareness about? Is it a local, regional, national or international issue?

Now get the group to prioritise these issues. Explain that all of the issues are obviously important to the group, but that the issues they rank in the top 3 are the ones that they will go on to consider in more detail.

Depending on the number of people you have, this exercise could be done as one single group or in small groups who, once they have made their choices, come together and compare answers / negotiate to come up with one list.

(30 minutes)

Identify the top 3 issues or situations that they have decided they want to do something about. Divide them into 3 groups and give each group a copy of the prompt sheet. Ask young people to discuss these questions with the rest of the group and take notes. They will need to present their answers to the rest of the group at the end of the exercise.

(20 minutes)

Come back into one group and hear each group make their case for why their issue should be the campaign.

Explain to the group that when deciding what they want to campaign on, it's important to consider if some key things which can make it easier to win a campaign exist in this particular situation. Thinking about the discussion they have just had, ask them:

▷ Have they been able to identify an obvious problem?

▷ Can they think of a solution to that problem?

▷ Do they think that they can show that solving that problem will help people?

▷ Is it something that other people will have heard about and / or be interested in?

If the group can answer yes to all or most of these questions, then there is more of a chance of their campaign being successful. If the answer is no, maybe the group needs to think again about what it is they want to campaign on.

Get the group to come to a consensus on what their campaign issue is going to be.

(30 minutes)

4A. Prompt sheet: Defining the Issue

Why are we choosing this as a campaign?

What are the main issues?

Who do they affect?

Who has the power to change these issues?

Do most people know about this issue?

What do we hope will change as a result of our campaign?

What could be the goal of the campaign?

SAMPLE SESSION PLANS AND ACTIVITY SHEETS

5. CHOOSING A CAMPAIGN GOAL[1]

Aim: For young people to think about how achievable their goals are and to refine their ideas from broad concepts into specific ideas.

Time: 45 minutes

What You Need:

Post it notes

Plan:

Split the group up into smaller groups and make sure everyone has a post-it note. Each person should write down what they think the goal of the campaign should be. In other words, what are they asking for? Encourage them to make it as specific as possible. For example, it shouldn't just be about "improving public transport", but something more specific like "reduced fares for under 16s".

Get each group to draw the following diagram on a piece of flipchart paper:

```
                Easy to achieve
Specific Goal ─────────────────── Broad Goal
                Difficult to achieve
```

Ask each member of the group to place their post it note on the diagram. The location of the note should be based on how specific the goal is (horizontal) and how easy it is to achieve (vertical). Any goals that are the same or similar can be stuck together.

Ask the group to discuss the goal and where it's been placed as it's put up. Encourage them to think about:

▷ Whether it is too broad. Will that make it difficult to focus?

▷ Is it clear what is being asked for?

In one group, get the young people to debate what the overall goal should be, based on what they have written. Their ideas can be combined and refined to come up with the most suitable goal. Agreement can be reached by consensus or by voting on it.

[1] Written by Dan Moxon, Regional Participation Officer, North West Regional Youth Work Unit

6. CHOOSING WHO TO FOCUS ON

Aim: For young people to identify which people and / or organisations they need to focus on as part of their campaign and why.

Time: 50 minutes

What You Need:

Activity Sheet
Influence map
Pens
Flip chart paper

Plan:

Write the group's agreed campaign goal up on a piece of flip chart paper. Ask them to come up with a list of any people or organisations they can think of who they need to involve in their campaign. Write these up on the flipchart.

(10 minutes)

Then divide into smaller groups and allocate each some of the people or organisations they have just identified.

Hand out the activity sheet to each group and ask them to complete it in relation to their allocated people / organisations.

Prompt questions:

▷ Why do they think it's important to focus on those particular groups?

▷ What do they want them to do as part of this campaign?

▷ What influence does this person / organisation have – can they make decisions, or do you want to involve them as supporters?

▷ Are they likely to be friends of your campaign or opponents?

Come back into one group and discuss what they have come up with.

(20 minutes)

Use this information to help the group complete the influence map.

(20 minutes)

INFLUENCE MAP

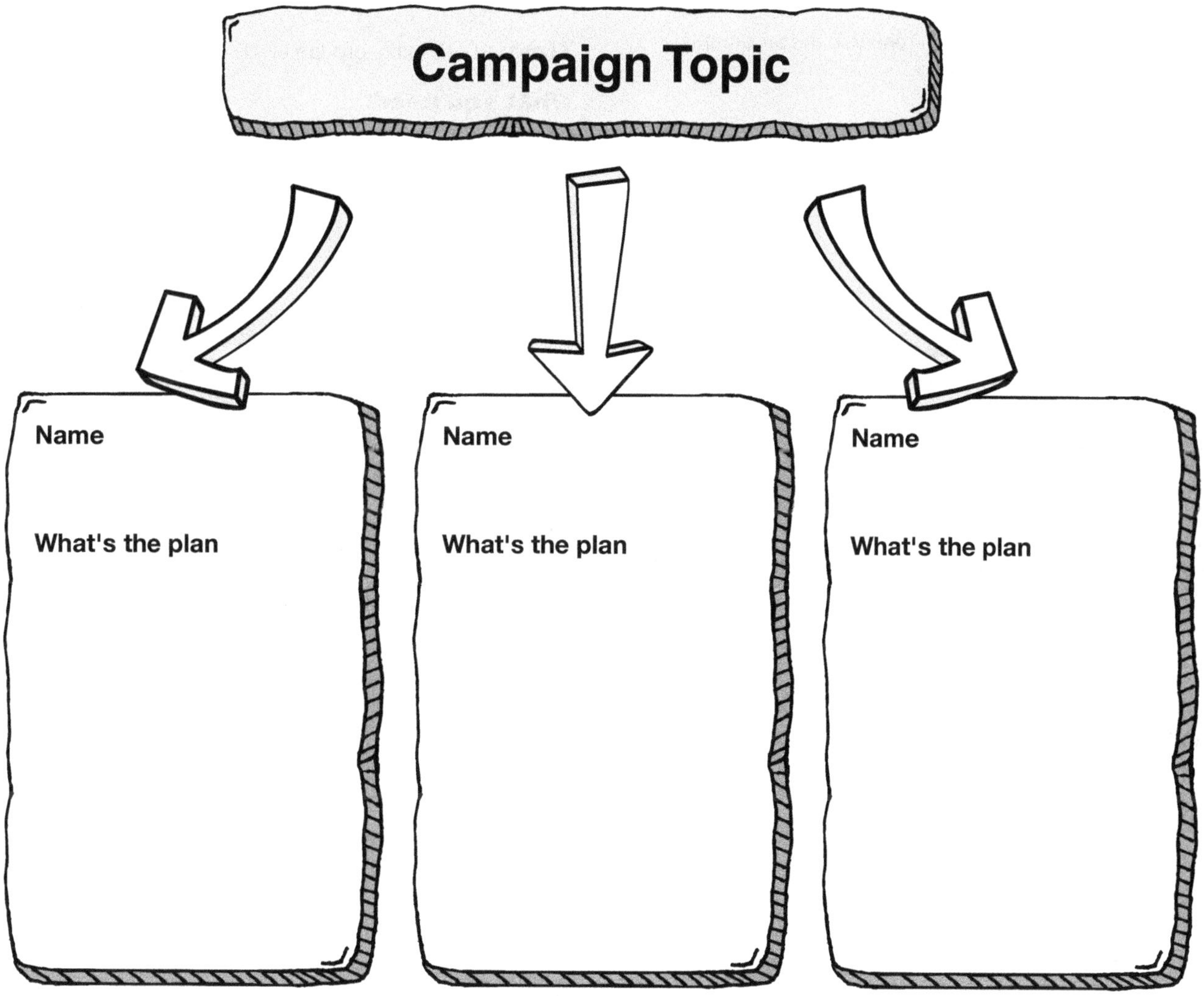

Campaign Topic

Name

What's the plan

Name

What's the plan

Name

What's the plan

Sample Session Plans and Activity Sheets

SAMPLE SESSION PLANS AND ACTIVITY SHEETS

7. DEBATING THE ISSUE

Aim: For young people to rehearse the arguments for / against their campaign.

Time: 45 minutes

What you need:
Pens / paper to take notes if needed.

Plan:

Select an issue for the group to discuss – it could be their campaign issue, a specific aspect of their campaign, or something else entirely.

Divide the group into two teams – Team Journalist and Team Interviewee. Explain that those in Team Journalist need to be convinced of the issue, whilst those in Team Interviewee will be doing the convincing. In their teams, each group should prepare the arguments they are going to use / second guess what the other team might counter with.

(15 minutes)

Ask each team to select one person who will then go up and debate with a representative from the other team. Alternatively, members from each team could be paired up with members from the other team to debate the issue in pairs.

(15 minutes)

Once they have had a chance to debate the issue, discuss with the group what worked / didn't work in convincing the other team of their arguments.

(15 minutes)

Note: instead of making the debate between a journalist and an interviewee, you could choose a particular target of the group's campaign – e.g. local council / MP – instead and make the debate between them and the campaign group.

8. BALLOON[2]

Aim: To help the group plan their campaign / a specific piece of work

Time: 30-45 mins, groups of 4-8 people

What you need:
Post-it notes
Flipchart
Pens
Balloon template

Thinking of the aim of their campaign, get participants to write or draw ideas on post-its and stick them on the relevant bit of the flipchart. Clarify ideas and group similar ones before moving on to the next topic.

1. On the balloon – issues and factors that will be needed for the proposal to Fly – their visions and ideas

2. In the basket – write the names of people or organisations who can help and support your aims

3. Ropes – what will hold it back, before the balloon/ project has started?

4. Clouds – what could push the balloon off course? (once the project has started)

5. Making it fly – above the balloon write factors that will make things happen and work

[2] Taken from Unite Participation's Essentials: Participation

BALLOON TEMPLATE

Sample Session Plans and Activity Sheets

SAMPLE SESSION PLANS AND ACTIVITY SHEETS

9. DECIDING ON YOUR MESSAGE

Aim: For young people to learn about the importance of having a clear message as part of their campaign.

Time: 2 hours

What you need:

Pens
Paper
Flipcharts

Plan:

Step 1

Explain that every campaign seeking to achieve change conveys some sort of message. If you do not put some thought into what message you wish to convey, there is the danger people will make assumptions themselves as to what you are trying to achieve. Therefore being absolutely clear what your overall message is will be absolutely crucial to your campaign. The message you convey will be up against the messages conveyed by those opposed to your campaign.

Divide people up into groups. Each group will look at a specific aspect of the message and write-up their conclusions on flipcharts

Group 1 – Discuss who are the people you need to know about your campaign. This could include specific groups within the general public as well working out who might make the decisions (such as elected politicians) that could allow your campaign to succeed. Who do you need to agree with and convince. Who might be opposed to your proposals? These are the audiences for your campaign.

Group 2 – Discuss what the strengths of the campaign are. What might help it succeed?

Group 3 – Discuss what the potential weaknesses of the campaign are. Why might it fail?

Step 2

Get each group to report back its findings. Allow time for questions and discussion. Do people agree with what each group has come up with? Has anything been missed out? Display the flipcharts prominently.

Step 3

At this point you could divide each of the three groups into three and create new groups comprising each a third from the previous groups.

Get each of the new groups to start crafting the message for the campaign from what they have learned. This should be written up on a flipchart

Top Tip: Messages should be no more than a paragraph in length explaining in some detail and clearly what you are proposing. They do not need to be just a slogan or catchphrase at this stage, though some slogans may emerge that you might want to record for subsequent campaign stages.

Try to answer some of the points or questions raised in Step 1, in order to ensure your message can convince the audiences it needs to appeal to.

Step 4

The three groups should report back what they suggest as the message of the campaign. There should be time for questions and discussion. The aim should be to combine the best elements of the three sets of conclusions into a single message. Hopefully this should arrive by consensus as the proposals are likely to be relatively similar. However do not be afraid to put some elements to a vote if people cannot all agree. However the main point should be that the message should unite everyone in the campaign, so consensus at this stage would be helpful.

10. WHAT MAKES A GOOD SLOGAN?

Aim: For young people to learn about what makes a good slogan.

Time: 1 hour

What you need:

Pens, paper, examples of adverts

Plan:

Explain that, having decided what your message is, you need to express it in a simple way to ensure the maximum number of people know what it is. This can be achieved through developing a campaign slogan. A slogan is a simple statement as to why people should support your campaign.

Step 1

Divide the young people into small groups. It is probably best to have at least 3-4 people, so that groups collectively have enough confidence to come up with a slogan and are able to present it to other groups.

Step 2

Ask each group to take the previously agreed message and think how it can be expressed in a short sentence. Groups are allowed to propose more than one slogan – especially if they are aiming that slogan at a specific group that needs to be influenced. Each group should be asked to present their slogan to the other groups.

Tips for the groups

People should think in terms of how the slogan would look if it were expressed as a still photo.

People should think about how it might be expressed if it were a TV or radio advert. Use examples of recent adverts as well as long-standing photos from advertising to give people ideas.

People should think of the audiences identified in the messaging exercise when drawing up slogans. There may be a need to develop slogans that are aimed at specific groups of people.

Step 3

After each group has presented its slogan and answered questions or heard comments, get them to vote on preferred slogans.

Firstly people should vote on the best slogan from each group. Each of these will go in the final group so each group is represented in the final decision.

Secondly all the remaining slogans for each group will be voted on one by one. Slogans that fail to secure half the votes of those present will be eliminated.

Step 4

The final shortlist of slogans will then be voted on to decide which one is to be the principal slogan. Other slogans that poll well could be used with some of the specific audiences identified during the message development exercise.

11. £5 NOTE

Aim: For young people to practice the art of persuasion.

Time: 20 minutes

What you need:

£5 note

Plan:

Place a £5 note in the middle of the group. Explain that everyone in the group will get 30 seconds to explain why they should get it for their cause / campaign. They can use the 30 seconds how they want and the group will vote on who to give the money to once everyone has had their turn.

Once the vote has been taken, discuss with the group their motives for voting. What was it that convinced them about what was said? What techniques were effective? Did they learn anything that they could use to help them promote their campaign?

Note: instead of getting the group to argue for their cause, you could get them to argue for an entirely unrelated issue, simply to practice techniques for trying to sell something / an idea to other people. Explain that they can do whatever they want (including lie) in their 30 seconds to try and win people round.

SAMPLE SESSION PLANS AND ACTIVITY SHEETS

12. STEPS TO THE FUTURE

Aim: For young people to identify what steps they could take to turn their ideas into action.

Time: 1 hour plus

What you need:

Flipchart paper
Pens
Footsteps template
Camera
Post it notes

Note: 10 years is used here as the suggested amount of time to think about, but this can be changed depending on the group / the issue.

Plan:

Stick two pieces of paper on the wall – one saying '2010' and one saying '2020'. Leave plenty of space between them so that the group can add their ideas.

Ask the group how they feel about their campaign issue at the moment. What's the first word that comes into their head when they think about it? What is it that they like / don't like? How would they describe the issue to someone who doesn't know much about it?

Get someone to scribble everyone's thoughts down on a piece of paper, from single words to whole sentences, and stick them next to the sign that says '2010'.
(15 minutes)

Now ask the group to do the same for 2020. How would they like to describe their issue in 2020?

How has what they don't like changed? How have their favourite things got even better? What are the words they would like to be associated with the issue in ten years time?

How would they like to describe the issue / campaign in 2020 to someone who hasn't heard about it?

Again, scribble it all down and stick the notes next to the '2020' sign.
(15 minutes)

Now it's time for the footprints. Take a couple of minutes quietly to think about how you could get from where the group sees they are now in 2010 to the place that they group want to be in 2020. This could be action by individuals, communities, businesses, local authorities, a combination or something else completely.

Think about:

▷ What changes need to be made?

▷ Which people do we need to pay more attention to?

▷ What should stay the same?

▷ What attitudes need to change?

▷ What technology do we need?

▷ Who needs to be involved?

When someone's ready, they can go ahead and write an idea down on one of the 'footprints', then stick it on the wall somewhere between 2010 and 2020.

What you should end up with is the beginnings of an action plan – where things are, where the group wants things to be and some sense of how they are going to get there.
(30 minutes)

This exercise can be extended by getting the group to go out into the community and take pictures or videos of things they particularly like or don't like at the moment to help illustrate their plan. This can then be used as "evidence", for example, if the group decides to campaign on changing something specific within their community.

12A. FOOTPRINTS TEMPLATE

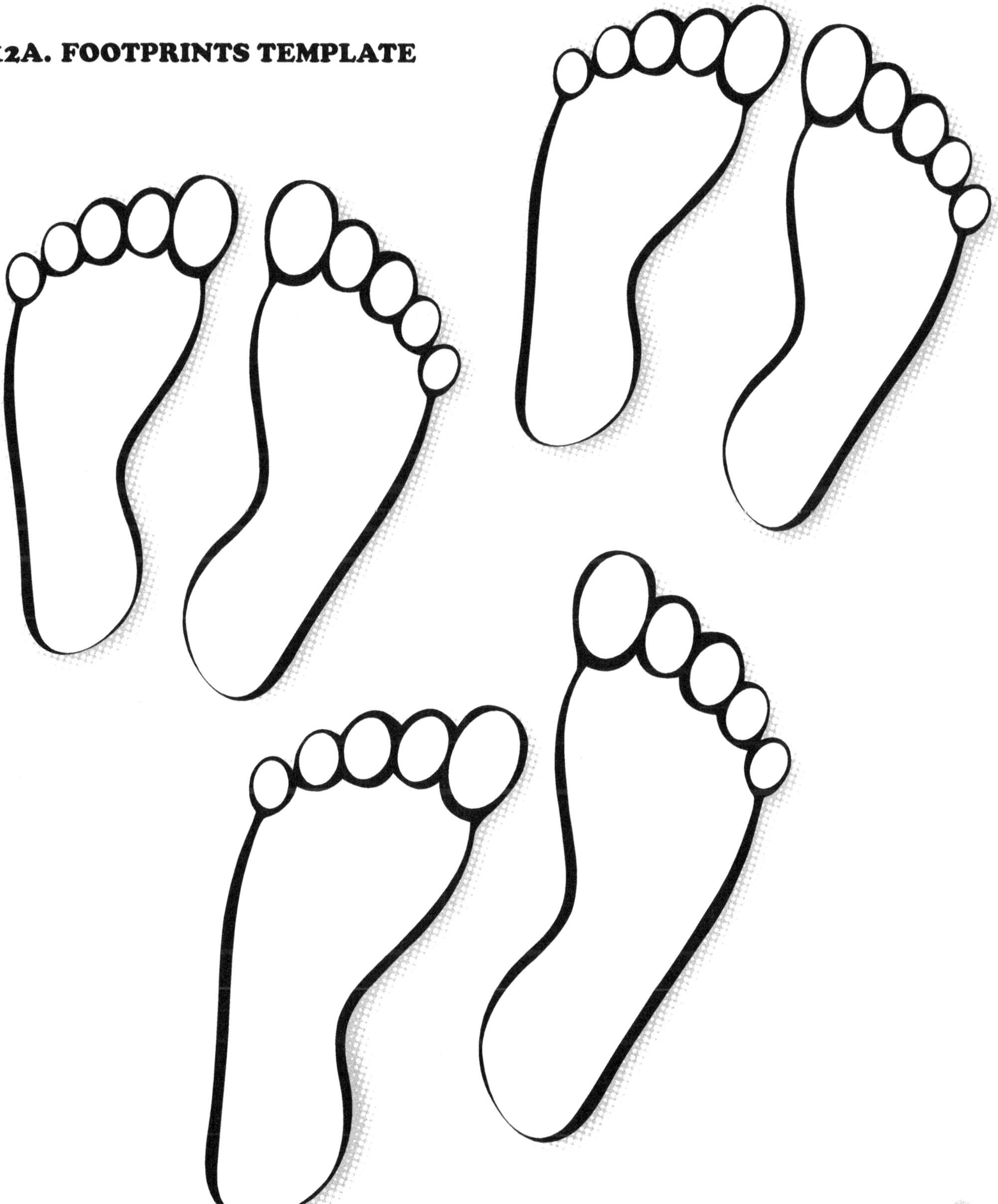

SAMPLE SESSION PLANS AND ACTIVITY SHEETS

13. PLANNING A CAMPAIGN

Aim: For young people to consider issues of message and communication when marketing their campaign.

Time: 40 minutes

What you need:
Case study
Paper
Pens

Plan:

Explain to the group that how they choose to promote their campaign will depend on a few different factors. Ask them what they think these might be:

▷ Who you are trying to influence

▷ Where they stand on the issue

▷ What methods they are most likely to respond to

▷ What stage of the campaign they are at

Divide into 3 groups. Each group is given the same campaign scenario, but has to market the campaign to a different audience. The idea is to get them to look at issues of message and communication – what works / doesn't.

(20 minutes)

Come back into one group and go through what the different groups have come up with. Questions to prompt discussion:

▷ Why have they chosen those people to influence?

▷ How can they help the campaign?

▷ Why did they choose the methods they did?

▷ At what stage during their campaign would they use these methods?

▷ What problems did they foresee?

▷ Why?

▷ What could be done to overcome these issues?

▷ How did it feel to do this exercise?

▷ Was it helpful in getting them to think about how to break a campaign down?

(20 minutes)

13A. PLANNING A CAMPAIGN SCENARIO

Your local town council has recently decided to ban young people from the shopping centre at weekends. You have decided to launch a campaign against this decision. You now need to plan your campaign, thinking specifically about how you will focus on the **young people / adults / decision makers** in your local area.

Things to consider:

▷ Who do you need to convince and why?

▷ What is your message going to be?

▷ What methods are you going to use to convince them to back your campaign?

▷ Why have you chosen to use those methods?

▷ What problems might you come up against in your campaign?

▷ How could you avoid / overcome those?

14. ACTION PLANNING

Aim: For participants to carry out a SWOT analysis of their campaign and use this to inform their action planning.

Time: 1 hour

What you need:
SWOT analysis
Action plan pro-forma

Plan:

Explain to the group that when they are planning their campaign, it is important to think about not only the things they can do well, but also any difficulties they may encounter along the way. Hand out the SWOT analysis and tell them that you want them to fill this out with reference to their campaign.

Explain that strengths and weaknesses are usually things that are internal to their group, whereas opportunities and threats are likely to be external factors. Depending on the numbers, this exercise can be carried out in one group or in smaller groups, who then come together and compare what they have written. What are the similarities / differences in their perceptions? What are the key themes to emerge?
(25 minutes)

Explain to the group that the SWOT analysis should help to give them a broad overview of the key issues that are likely to affect their campaign and that the next Action Planning exercise will help them to break down the campaign into key tasks. They should try and come up with some very specific ideas and steps that can be taken. Emphasise that it is important to be realistic about what can be achieved and when.

Go through the action plan with the group, to ensure that there are clear deadlines and allocated roles.
(25 minutes)

Finish off the session by going round the group and asking them to commit to one specific action they will take before the next meeting / a specified point.
(10 minutes)

14A. ACTION PLAN PRO-FORMA

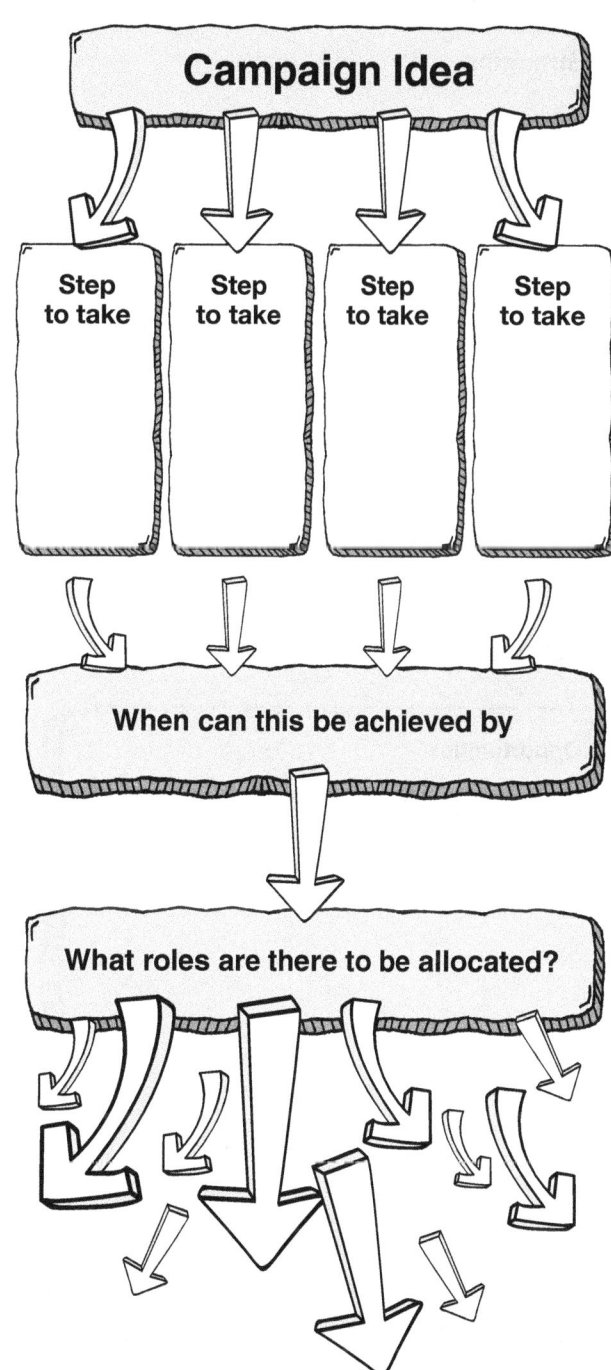

Sample Session Plans and Activity Sheets

SAMPLE SESSION PLANS AND ACTIVITY SHEETS

14B. S.W.O.T. ANALYSIS

15. TEAM BUILDING[3]

Aim: To encourage group communication and team work

Time: 15 minutes

What you need:
Nothing

Ask group to stand in a circle shoulder to shoulder. The circle should then put both hands in the air, so that they are pointing to the opposite side of the circle. Ask the group to take baby steps until the circle gets smaller and smaller. They should then grab someone else's hands. Once everyone is holding another hand, ask the group to untangle themselves without breaking the chain. It works best if the group work together and unchain themselves section by section.

[3] Taken from Unite Participation's Essentials: Participation

16. WHAT I WANT TO ACHIEVE

Aim: For young people to think about what they are good at and what they bring to the group and to identify any areas in which they feel they would like support.

Time: 40 minutes

What you need:
Activity sheet
Pens

Plan:

Explain to the group that everyone will have their own skills and qualities that they bring to the campaign. Thinking about what those are will help them to build a more effective team and make sure people are getting the most from their involvement with the group.

Give each young person a copy of the activity sheet and ask them to work their way around the sheet, recording what they want to get out of their involvement in the campaign and how they can get the most out of it.

Give them around 15 minutes to do this.

Then split the groups into pairs and get them to talk to each other about what they've put. Why have they put what they have? Did they find it hard to do? Have they written anything that surprised them?
(10 minutes)

Come back into one group and discuss what they have put. Questions to prompt discussion could include:

- How did they find completing the activity sheet?
- Did they enjoy doing it or not?
- Did they learn anything about themselves from filling it in?
- What kind of different strengths are there across the group?
- What can they learn from this that will help them to work better together as a group?

(15 minutes)

Sample Session Plans and Activity Sheets

SAMPLE SESSION PLANS AND ACTIVITY SHEETS

16A. WHAT I WANT TO ACHIEVE ACTIVITY SHEET

- What I can do to overcome what's stopping me from achieving those goals...
- Things that might stop me from achieving those goals...
- What I want to get out of my involvement with the campaign is...
- 3 things I would like to do during the campaign are...
- I got involved with the campaign because...
- 3 things I would like to get better at...
- 3 things I am good at...
- I would like to learn how to...
- To achieve this I need to...

17. LOBBYING – APPROACHING COUNCIL OFFICERS/COUNCILLORS/MPS

Aim: To learn about how to lobby decision makers effectively and practice lobbying skills.

Time: 1-2 hours

What you need:
Pens
Paper
Flipchart

Plan:

Ask the group if they know what lobbying means and what it involves.

Explain that lobbying is a way of seeking to explain your campaign and its message to those who may be in a position to decide on the issue or influence decisions. Lobbying is a structured approach to getting your campaign and its message across to those people who can help you make a difference.

Step 1

Divide participants up into small groups. They will need to identify who needs to be lobbied, drawing from the list of potential audiences that were drawn up for the messaging exercise. Each group should also decide what outcomes they want to achieve from the lobbying.

Tips

People who might be appropriate to lobby include, for example, local Councillors over the provision of a local facility, or it might be Members of Parliament or Members of the European Parliament regarding National or European Policy.

Potential outcomes that lobbying might seek to achieve could include making politicians and decisions makers aware of the problem, then seeking a response from them, or it might go as far as seeking a formal decision from them.

Step 2

Report back on the potential people to lobby based on the campaign and the message that has previously been agreed. Agree what are the outcomes that need to be achieved and the priority order. For example, if the issue is not that well known, achieving awareness may be the initial key priority.

Step 3

Having agreed the specific group to lobby, divide people into three groups to prepare for a role play.

Group 1 – Will be the team who lobby on behalf of everybody. They need to decide how they will present their message and to whom.

Group 2 – Will play the role of the people to be lobbied. They need to decide who will be their spokesperson and what their initial view on the issue is on behalf of the Council, or Government. They might want to look at the weaknesses identified in the messaging exercise and put the case of the authorities.

Group 3 – Will play members of the public. They will observe and indicate which side put their case best. They need to decide how they will score the issue. Issues they might want to consider are both the strengths and weaknesses of the message, how expensive the issue might be as well as score how each side put their message across.

Step 4

The actual lobbying will be presented as a formal meeting, with Group 1 sitting at a table putting their case, with Groups 2 responding and Group 3 acting as an audience and taking notes.

Step 5

At the end of the role play, ask Group 3 to indicate how both Groups came across and which side put their case the best. Groups 1 and 2 will be also asked to comment on how each other came across. The exercise can be repeated, allocating different roles to each group, so that young people all have a chance to practice lobbying skills.

Step 6

Invite some general discussion to identify what was learned so the campaign, its message and slogans can be improved further.

SAMPLE SESSION PLANS AND ACTIVITY SHEETS

18. DEALING WITH THE MEDIA

Aim: For participants to look at what makes something newsworthy and learn skills for dealing with the media.

Time: About 1 hour

What you need:
Selection of recent newspaper front pages
Flipchart paper
Pens
Scenario cards

Plan:

Explain to the group that the media can be a very powerful ally in raising the profile of their campaign, if they can manage to secure the coverage they would like.

Ask them what they think news is. According to Mark Twain, news is "history in its first and best form".

Where do we see news? TV, papers, hear it on the radio, internet etc.

(5 minutes)

Divide into smaller groups and distribute a selection of recent front page articles from newspapers. Ask the groups to go through these articles and decide on why they think that story made it on to the front page. What is it that marks it out / makes people want to read it?

Come back into one group and go through what they thought. What does it tell them about what makes something newsworthy?

It needs to be shocking, original, unusual, topical, relevant and of genuine interest to people.

(15 minutes)

When during their campaign are they likely to need to contact the media?

- When there's an important vote or meeting coming up
- To raise awareness of what they are trying to achieve
- To reply to something that's been written or said about their campaign
- To publicise an event they're organising

Explain that if they want to get media attention, more often than not they are going to need to convince a journalist who is probably very busy and not that interested, so they're going to have to find a way to "sell" what they are doing, if they're going to get noticed. One way to do this might be contacting them by phone.

Divide the group into pairs and give each a scenario (or use a real life example from their own campaign).

One member of the pair is a journalist and the other has to convince them of the merits of their campaign. They have one minute to do this. Then swap roles and repeat.

Come back into one group and discuss how they felt about doing that. Did anyone come up with something to really grab the attention of the journalist?

(10 minutes)

Explain that they might also need to generate interest by writing an article or issuing a press release. Ask the group what they think a press release is:

- It's written
- It's news
- You can e-mail it to papers / magazines / radio and TV stations
- Journalists will get a lot of them, so yours won't be that special to them

Divide into groups and give them a scenario, containing basic information about an event. Depending on how many people there are in the group you could get one group to write a release for print media, another for the television or radio and a third to turn the information into an article for the local paper.

(20 minutes)

18A. "SELLING IN"

You are holding a public meeting to discuss the planned closure of your local community centre. The meeting is next week and will be attended by members of groups who currently use the centre, such as the youth club, Parent and Toddlers group and the Tenants' Association. The local councillor will also be at the meeting. You would like someone from the local paper to come along to the meeting.

You are organising a day of action at your local school / college to raise awareness about climate change. You have invited speakers from organisations like Greenpeace and you will be having a green fayre during the lunch break. You want some publicity for the event ahead of the day and would like the local radio station to help you with this.

As part of your campaign to improve a local playground, you have been running a survey to find out what the community thinks and you have now collated the results and written them up in a report. You would like to get some publicity for your findings from the local TV station.

You are running a campaign to promote a better image of young people. As part of this you are holding a party organised by young people for the residents of an old people's home. You would like the local media to cover this event.

18B. WRITING A PRESS RELEASE

Scenario 1

You need to write a press release based on the following information:

Background Information

Event: Anti-racist youth football tournament

Date: Saturday 20 July

Venue: The Wreck

Time: 11am-4pm

Key Audience: 13-19 year olds. Separate tournaments for young men and young women.

Organised by: The Unity Youth Club

Special guests: The tournament will be opened by the Mayor and the medals will be awarded by a local Championship footballer

What's happening: 5-a-side football tournament, coaching sessions run by the Sports Development Workers, music, information stalls, including Show Racism the Red Card, and refreshments.

Cost: Free

Registration: Teams must register by 15 July as there is limited space. Register at onegame.net

For further details: Contact Unity Youth Club 0867 443232

Scenario 2

You need to write a press release based on the following information:

Background Information

Event: Demonstration on climate change and rally in Hyde Park

Date: Saturday 20 July

Venue: Meet Embankment tube 12pm

Time: 12-5pm

Key Audience: Open to all

Organised by: Our World campaign group, Greenpeace, Friends of the Earth

Special guests: Speakers at the rally will include politicians and religious leaders.

What's happening: March through central London, ending up at a rally in Hyde Park, with stalls, music and refreshments

Cost: Free

Registration: Not required

For further details: Contact Our World at ourworld.org.uk or call 01023 456 777

Sample Session Plans and Activity Sheets

SAMPLE SESSION PLANS AND ACTIVITY SHEETS

19. NEGOTIATING AND INFLUENCING

Aim: For young people to practice skills in negotiating and influencing

Time: 90 minutes

What you need:

Pack of cards

Flipchart paper

Pens

Feet cut outs

Planning a Negotiation sheet

Negotiation scenario

Plan:

Introduction (5 minutes)

Explain to the group that when they are working with others there will be times when they have to compromise on what they want to achieve or try and win others to their point of view. This is known as negotiation and influencing.

This session looks at what the key ingredients to ensuring success when you have to negotiate or seek to influence others.

Pairs activity (10 minutes)

Divide the participants into pairs, and give each pair four cards (two per participant). Then go round to each pair and place a fifth card on the floor in between each pair, inform the pairs that they are not to pick up the card yet.

Once you have given every pair their fifth card, inform the pairs that they have to decide between themselves who will have the additional fifth card. They have to try and persuade their partner why they should have the extra card rather than their partner; they have no more than five minutes to do this.

After five minutes, bring all the pairs back together to form one large group. Ask the participants the following questions,

1. Did any pairs come to a decision on who should have the additional card?

2. Were any pairs still discussing who should have the fifth card?

When participants answer either question, ask them either how they came to a decision or why they were still undecided? The thing to bring out is the fact that they needed to have a reason for agreeing or disagreeing with their partner. This is something that you will come back to after the small group activity.

Idea storm (10 minutes)

Ask participants the following questions and write their suggestions onto flipchart paper:

1. What is negotiation?

2. In what situations would they be required to negotiate (specifically in relation to the campaign)?

Explain that negotiation is about "getting agreement through discussion and compromising". It differs from influence which is about leading or trying to control something or someone.

Negotiating broken down (20 minutes)

Refer back to the activity with the cards at the start of the session; remind participants that they all had reasons as to why they agreed with their partner who would have the fifth card or why they were undecided.

Inform the participants that what we are now going to look at what they think are the vital steps you need to take to come to such decisions.

Divide the participants into smaller groups of 4/5 people. Explain to the participants that as with anything there are steps that you need to take to be successful when negotiating and seeking to influence others.

Inform the smaller groups that they need to think about what the steps are to being successful. Distribute a number of large cut out feet and pens to each of the smaller groups and inform them that they are to write what they feel the steps are to successfully negotiate and influence others.

Inform the groups that when they have finished their discussions they are to lay out their large feet in a line, placing the feet in the order of the steps that they need to take to be effective negotiators and influencers.

Ask one person from each of the smaller groups to explain their steps, reading out the stages their group decided on.

Steps to effective influencing

Talk through the four key steps to influencing:

1. Set your objective – identify what it is you want to achieve

2. Identify the other person's needs – find out what it is the other person wants to get

3. Identify what you will give up – know what you are willing to give up or compromise as well as what you are unwilling to give up

4. Prepare to meet with the other person – it's the only way to!

Relate the four stages to the lines of feet on the floor containing the participants' thoughts on the steps required to be successful when negotiating and influencing.

Inform the participants that when they are negotiating they should always:

- Aim high – try to achieve the best that you can

- Reluctantly give concessions – it is important to drive a hard bargain

There are some other strategies that you could use:

- **There is only one way** – your solution is the only solution

- **Can we break this down** – some things are too big to agree straight away and will need to be broken into smaller decisions

- **Do you know who I am?** Relying on status rather than skill. This requires you to be dominant and forceful

- **I have to check with other people first** – Can't make a decision on the spot, you have to go back to others

- **Good cop/ bad cop** – when one person is very critical and aggressive; the other is sweet and easygoing. The underlying message is that if you don't do this then something unpleasant might happen.

- **Extremes** – you propose something extreme in order to get the small gain you actually want

- **Ultimatum** – this is our last and final offer – can be risky if the other people decide against your position. It is useful when you are paying for a service as you can threaten to go somewhere else for that service

- **Clockwatching** – using time helps create a real sense of urgency and force an agreement. For example saying that there is only 30 minutes to get a decision otherwise nothing can happen for the next three weeks

- **Repackaging** – taking something you have already tried to negotiate for and presenting it in a difficult way

- **We both like vegetables but you like tomatoes and I like carrots** – start from the position of what you agree on

Inform participants that negotiations are usually done by a team or group rather than being left to an individual. Individual's however, may try to influence group negotiations or decisions this usually occurs in meetings.

Negotiation and influencing skills (40 minutes)

Divide the group into two smaller groups. Give each group the scenario explaining their different views. Inform the groups that they have to negotiate the situation. Give each group a copy of the Planning a Negotiation sheet and ask them to use this to prepare for their negotiation.

Sample Session Plans and Activity Sheets

SAMPLE SESSION PLANS AND ACTIVITY SHEETS

After ten minutes, bring the two smaller groups together and ask them to start negotiating. Tell them they have 20 minutes to reach a compromise.

At the end of that time, use the following points as a guide to debrief the activity:

- Ask them generally how they felt about the outcome
- Ask them what they have learnt
- If they did it again would they do it differently?
- What was realistic?
- What was unrealistic?

Summary and close (5 minutes)

Review the session's content, reminding participants that an important aspect of being successful when negotiating and influencing others is to aim for the ideal of a win: win situation, which is in the best interest of both organisations and parties. The key is to identify a better way of doing something rather than "my way" or "your way".

Remind participants that negotiation and influencing is an art and like any other skill, needs practice.

Summarise the session using the following points:

- Remember the four key steps
- Find out the other person's views on the subject
- Work out your objective
- Rehearse your points of view/ argument
- Use a number of strategies

Emphasise that it is important to know your boundaries i.e. your bottom line. This requires clear roles and responsibilities which maybe delegated to a group or an individual.

19A. NEGOTIATING SKILLS SHEET

Aspect of Negotiation	Notes
Goals	
Trades	
Alternatives	
Relationships	
Expected outcomes	
The consequences	
Power	
Possible solutions	

19B. HOW SHOULD THE COUNCIL SPEND ITS MONEY?

Team 1

You are the youth representatives on your Community Forum. Your local council has allocated £10,000 to do up a local park and the Community Forum is responsible for deciding how to spend the money.

The park has become very run down recently and there have been problems with people using it for drinking and taking drugs. There is a football pitch in the park at the moment but no-one uses it much in the winter because there is no lighting in the park. There is a small children's play area, but the equipment is old and parents don't like to take their children there due to the people drinking and taking drugs.

You have spoken to the young people who use the park about their priorities, and based on your research you would like to spend the money on the following:

Improving the play area	£5,000.00
Lighting for the football pitch	£2,000.00
Benches for people to sit on	£1,000.00
A skateboard ramp	£2,000.00
TOTAL	**£10,000.00**

The other group on the board think that the money should be spent on turning it into a community garden and allotments.

Team 2

How are you going to negotiate with them to get the best result for both of you?

You are the adult representatives on your Community Forum. Your local council has allocated £10,000 to do up a local park and the Community Forum is responsible for deciding how to spend the money.

The park has become very run down recently and there have been problems with people using it for drinking and taking drugs. There is a football pitch in the park at the moment but no-one uses it much in the winter because there is no lighting in the park. There is a small children's play area, but the equipment is old and parents don't like to take their children their due to the people drinking and taking drugs.

You believe that the park as it is has become more trouble than it is worth and you want to spend the money on turning it into a community garden and allotments.

The other team will argue that the money needs to be spent on keeping it as a park doing it up.

How are you going to negotiate the best result for both of you?

Sample Session Plans and Activity Sheets

SAMPLE SESSION PLANS AND ACTIVITY SHEETS

20. PRACTICING PUBLIC SPEAKING

Aim: To enable participants to develop and practice skills of speaking with confidence in public.

Time: 70 minutes

What you need:
A4 paper
Pens
Stopwatch
Speech template

Plan:

Explain to the group that all of them will have to make a speech or presentation in public at some point in their lives. For example, it might be at a meeting or an event where they are representing their campaign. Making a speech can be quite a frightening prospect, but with a little planning, preparation and practice there's no need to worry.
(5 minutes)

Explain to the group that it is not just about what you say, but how you say it that matters. Things like your body language (how you carry yourself) and your tone of voice are as important as the words that you use.

Divide them into small groups and give each group a pen and a piece of paper. Ask each group to draw a large circle on their paper and then tell them that they have to decide how much in terms of percentage each of the following matters during a speech:

- The words you use
- The tone of what you say
- How you use / hold your body – your body language

(5 minutes)

Ask the groups what they came up with? Who put which category first and what percentages did they have?

Explain to the group that according to some research done by Albert Mehrabian in 1971, the breakdown is approximately:

- Body language 55%
- Tone of your voice – 38%
- Words you use – 7%

Get them to test this out in pairs, by the different ways in which they can say / stand when saying a simple phrase, such as "I really like chocolate."
(10 minutes)

Explain that people don't always focus on what you say, but how you say them instead, so it will be important to think about non-verbal communication as well when you are speaking.

Highlight the importance of preparation in giving a good presentation, as they will need to make sure that what they are saying is accurate. Ask them to come up with a list of things that they think they need to take into account when planning. These include:

- Finding out who your audience is – as this will affect the type of language they use and your language
- Where will you be speaking? At a lectern, standing or sitting, large or small room?
- How many people will be there?
- How long have you got? It's usually better to keep it short and sweet – but you could break up your time, by using visual aids, video clips etc.
- Write your presentation / make some notes to speak from

Explain that the success of a presentation is about 10% delivery and 90% preparation.

So, how do they go about structuring their speech? Any ideas? Explain that:

- All presentations need a beginning, where you introduce yourself and what you're going to be talking about
- A middle – where you focus on 3 key aspects / themes related to the subject you're speaking on
- An end – where you sum up what you've said, including a closing remark or though
- Keep things in 3s – it focuses attention and makes it easier to remember what's being said

Key rule to remember: tell them what you're going to say, say it and then tell them what you've said.

Hand out a copy of the speech template to each member of the group. Explain that they are going to have to plan and give a 2 minute talk about a subject of their choice (something they feel comfortable talking about) and that they can use the template to help them with their planning. Give them 15-20 minutes to plan / practice their talks. Hand out stopwatches to help them judge the length.

Depending on the size of your group, you may want to keep them in smaller groups to give their speeches. At the end of each speech, ask the participant how they felt it went and invite other members of the group to give positive feedback – one thing done well / that was particularly good – nothing negative / point out where they could get better.
(40 minutes)

In one group, review the session and emphasise that they have all done really well.
(10 minutes)

20A. PLANNING YOUR PRESENTATION

Length of presentation/speech: minutes

Audience:

Venue:

Beginning
Say who you are and where you are from:

What are you talking about?

Middle
Point 1:

Point 2:

Point 3:

End
Summary of your three points:

Closing remarks:

Sample Session Plans and Activity Sheets

SAMPLE SESSION PLANS AND ACTIVITY SHEETS

21. RUNNING A PUBLIC MEETING

Aim: To get to grips with the act of planning, running and following up a public meeting

Time: 1-2 hours

What you need:
Pen
Paper

Plan:

Planning a meeting is actually fairly hard; even the best campaigners and politicians sometimes organise meetings where either no-one turns up, or nothing of any use comes from it.

This quick exercise enables you to turn an everyday conversation with a group of friends into a mock public meeting, following all the principles that a good public meeting should.

Quite simply, pick an issue to discuss (it could be anything from discussing what to do about Global Warming to – if you are going to be talking to a group of friends – what you should do the next weekend). Once you've got a group together, simply discuss it...

A few tips...

Use these basic tips to structure the exercise and help the group to plan their own public meeting.

Step 1: Building your audience

- Who do you want there? If it is about planning your weekend, invite your friends. If it is a more serious issue, think about both who you want to discuss it with and also, who's mind you might want to change

- Also, how are you going to get them to come? Does the meeting need to be somewhere everyone feels comfortable?

Step 2: Running the meeting

- Unless you want it to be a free-for-all, you will need to assign roles for different people. For example, someone will need to lead the debate to make sure everyone can contribute

- Also, if you want anything useful to come from the meeting, someone will need to make some notes. How will you choose these people?

Step 3: Making sure it counts

- What do you want to get out of the meeting? It isn't always possible to make everyone agree on the same thing, but think carefully about what you want

- If you just want to make sure everyone at the meeting knows you care about something, then you might not need to do anything else However, ideally you should have some 'actions' to take on. These 'actions' are things that people at the meeting have committed to do

- So, sticking with the same examples as before, these might be anything from a final decision on what to do the next weekend, or in the case of Global Warming, a commitment to do some research on a particular issue before having another meeting to decide what can be done

22. SETTING UP A FACEBOOK GROUP OR PAGE

Aim: For young people to learn how to plan and set up a Facebook Group or Page

Time: 1-2 hours

What you need:
Pens
Paper
Computer with internet access

Plan:

Explain to the group that setting up a Facebook Group is very simple – the key thing is to develop an effective one that will have a lot of members.

As many people involved in their campaign are likely to have used Facebook, the taking part in the following planning process is likely to help them develop their own group or page.

Divide into two groups and ask them to discuss the following issues:

- Decide on whether a page or a group would be best for the campaign
- Who is the group / page going to be aimed at? What is the likely audience?
- What do you want from the group / page? Is it just a place for people to signify their support and signpost people to a main website, or is it the campaign's main web based tool?
- How often will it need to be updated with new content?
- Who will take responsibility for being administrators and keep the group / page both up to date and active?
- How will they promote the group / page? Who will take responsibility for making this happen?
- What is a good name for the group / page, in view of what they have decided? Does it need to be serious or funny?

The two groups should then come together to present their findings and decide between the two of them what is the best approach.

Note: When supporting the group to plan how to use Facebook as part of their campaign, it can be useful to bear in mind the following points:

A page on Facebook is like advertising, as people can be fans of many pages. This means that you can have status updates appearing on people's feeds.

Groups are more powerful tools as you can use these to create events and email invites and get the event in people's calendar on Facebook.

Identify if any Facebook apps might be of use to your group or page – for example, survey tools, but many apps will also want to use you for advertising, so they might not be what you need for a campaign.

23. SETTING UP A TWITTER FEED

Aim: For young people to learn how to use Twitter as part of their campaign.

Time: 1 hour

What you need:
Pens
Paper
Computer with internet access

Plan:

Ask the group how many of them are already familiar with Twitter. How many of them use it already and what for? Ask them what they like about it.

Explain that a Twitter feed is simple to set up. The 140 character updates, are a simple way to tell other people about what you are up to without having to write large press releases or other documents.

Ask the group to think through how they could run a Twitter feed as part of their campaign. They will need to think about:

- Who is this going to be aimed at? What is the likely audience?
- How often will they update it? A twitter feed that is not updated will look as if the campaign is inactive. Who will take responsibility for being administrator and keep the group both up to date and active?
- How will you promote the group? Who will take responsibility for making this happen?

Sample Session Plans and Activity Sheets

SAMPLE SESSION PLANS AND ACTIVITY SHEETS

▷ What is a good name for the feed? Remember that is likely to be limited in terms of the number of characters you can use. If your organisation or campaign has a long name how can you shorten it or come with something serious or funny?

Note: Setting up the actual feed is simple. Go to **www.twitter.com** and register. It is a simple three step process, just asking for simple information. Setting up a simple web based campaign email first using Google, Yahoo or Live.com might make sense before you set up anything else, as if you already have a twitter feed yourself, you may create problems if you use your own personal email address.

Think about if you are going to run the twitter feed in conjunction with a Facebook page? Can you update both together? If so a website like **http://ping.fm/** might help here and save you time. Twitter and Facebook can also be added as links to your website, to make that more interesting if you do not change the content of that too much.

24. STARTING A BLOG

Aim: For young people to learn how to plan and set up their own campaign blog.

Time: 1 hour

What you need:
Pens
Paper
Computer with internet access

Plan:

Ask the group what they think a blog is. Explain that a blog is way of conveying thoughts and news. Often bloggers are single individuals expressing their views on things in general or on a specific subject area. However blogs can also be used by those campaigning as a group, so long as they are updated regularly.

To help them get started on planning their blog, ask the group to consider the following:

▷ Who is the blog going to be aimed at? What is the likely audience for it?

▷ Who will take responsibility for writing it? Is someone going to be the editor or chief blogger? Are you going to operate a rota of contributors?

▷ How will you promote the blog? Who will take responsibility for making this happen?

▷ How will it link to your other online activity, such as a standard website, Facebook or Twitter? Could you put all this information on a Facebook page? Is that the right approach?

▷ What will be the name of the blog? Often blogs have very memorable names to help people online remember they are out there

Note: There are a number of blogging websites. The easiest to set up quickly is: **http://www.blogger.com**

Setting it up takes just a few minutes, especially if the group has done the planning suggested above.

Thinking of a blog as a bit like a regular diary entry should help to remind the group that they have to regularly update it. If the group have weekly or monthly planning meetings, include the blog as a regular item to ensure it's being kept up to date.

Think news – blogs can be a regular source of local media information. One of the most avid readers of blogs, and often bloggers themselves, are local journalists. They use blogging to improve their writing and journalism skills. A good tip is to offer to swap a link with your blog and their blog to build a relationship with them.

25. CREATING AN ONLINE SURVEY

Aim: To plan and prepare a survey using Survey Monkey.

Time: 1 hour

What you need:

Pens

Paper

Computer with internet access

Plan:

Ask the group what they think the benefits of an online survey could be to their campaign. Explain that they can be used to:

▷ Gather information and opinions that help with the direction of the campaign, especially early on when you are formulating a message

▷ Provide a news item that sustains interest in your campaign

▷ Enable you to check whether your campaign is raising awareness

▷ Provide feedback later in the campaign in case you need to adjust any parts of it to make it more effective

They are also very simple to set up quickly, so they can often be an answer to "what do we do next" if you have reached a point in your campaign when you have tried most other things once.

The most well known online Survey system is Survey Monkey: **http://www.surveymonkey.com**

The "basic plan" is free and will enable the group to set up a survey, by following the simple list of instructions online. However, explain to the group that it will be important to be clear about exactly what it is they want to achieve with their survey. Ask them to consider the following questions:

▷ How does the survey fit in with the other activity they are planning?

▷ What is the objective of the survey? Is it for gathering information or raising awareness or both?

▷ What is the likely audience for the survey? Will some people be left out?

▷ Is online the only approach? Should it be replicated with offline pen and paper surveys

▷ Who will take responsibility for designing the survey? Perhaps you need a meeting to set out all the questions? Can the surveys you might be writing offline be adapted for this?

▷ Who will download the information collected and analyse it? Most online surveys do a lot of the number crunching for you, but you still need to think about how you present the information.

▷ Are they writing a report or a press release or even summarising it in a Twitter Feed or on a Facebook update?

▷ How will the survey be promoted? Who will take responsibility for making this happen? Is there a list of people's e-mail addresses it could be sent to?

Once they are clear about what they want to get from the survey and how they are going to use it, work with the group to use Survey Monkey to design their questionnaire.

SAMPLE SESSION PLANS AND ACTIVITY SHEETS

SAMPLE EVALUATION GRID

This can be adapted and used to review the progress of your campaign

Activity	W/C		W/C		W/C	
	Target	Actual	Target	Actual	Target	Actual
Supporters recruited						
Voters met						
Leaflets put out						
Calls made						
Promises of votes						
Meetings done						

CHALLENGES & TARGETS

Using this section

This section contains sample Youth Achievement Award challenges and Youth Challenge targets. They are divided into 4 main areas:

1. Introduction to campaigning

▷ **Bronze YAA Challenge/ Youth Challenge activities**

i. Take part in activities to explore what a campaign is and understand why young people might want to get involved in one.

▷ **Silver YAA Challenge / Youth Challenge Extra**

i. Help organise and run activities for young people to explore what a campaign is and what reasons there might be for getting involved in one.

▷ **Gold YAA Challenge**

i. Lead activities for young people to explore what a campaign is and help them to explore their reasons for getting involved in one.

2. Planning a campaign

▷ **Bronze YAA Challenge/ Youth Challenge activities**

i. Take part in activities to explore what makes a good campaign and understand how to plan one.

▷ **Silver YAA Challenge / Youth Challenge Extra**

i. Help run and organise activities for young people to explore what makes a good campaign and understand how to plan one.

▷ **Gold YAA Challenge**

i. Lead activities for young people to explore what makes a good campaign and understand how to plan one.

3. Doing it

▷ **Bronze YAA Challenge / Youth Challenge Activities**

Take part in activities that will help young people deliver their campaign.

▷ **Silver Challenge / Youth Challenge Extra Activities**

Help organise activities that will support young people to deliver their campaign.

▷ **Gold YAA Challenge**

i. Organise and lead activities for young people to enable them to run their campaign.

4. Shout about it

▷ **Bronze YAA Challenge / Youth Challenge Activities**

i. Take part in activities to learn about publicising your campaign.

▷ **Silver Challenge / Youth Challenge Extra Activities**

i. Help organise and run activities about publicising your campaign.

▷ **Gold YAA Challenge**

i. Organise and run activities to support young people to publicise their campaign.

Each section has sample ideas for activities, challenges and targets at Bronze / Youth Challenge, Silver / Youth Challenge Extra and Gold level Awards. A range of suggested session plans and activity sheets are included elsewhere in this toolkit to complement the suggested activities, challenges and targets.

This section should be used flexibly and activities, challenges and targets should be adapted to suit the needs of the group you are working with.

CHALLENGES & TARGETS

1. INTRODUCTION TO ACCREDITING CAMPAIGNING

Bronze YAA Challenge / Youth Challenge activities

Take part in activities to explore what a campaign is and understand why young people might want to get involved in one.

Possible targets:

▷ Take part in the What is a Campaign? exercise

▷ Take part in the Getting Your Voice Heard exercise

▷ Participate in a discussion about why it's important for young people to get involved in campaigns

▷ Take part in the Have YOUR say exercise

▷ Watch a short film made by a campaign group and take part in a discussion about what defines their campaign

▷ Take part in a workshop run by a campaign group

Silver YAA Challenge / Youth Challenge Extra

Help organise and run activities for young people to explore what a campaign is and what reasons there might be for getting involved in one.

Possible targets:

▷ Help to run the What is a Campaign? exercise

▷ Help facilitate the Getting Your Voice Heard exercise

▷ Help plan and lead a discussion about why it's important for young people to get involved in campaigns

▷ Help facilitate the Have YOUR say exercise

▷ Find a campaign film for the group to watch and help to facilitate a discussion about it.

▷ Do some research into campaign groups who could deliver a workshop.

Gold YAA Challenge

Lead activities for young people to explore what a campaign is and help them to explore their reasons for getting involved in one.

Possible targets:

▷ Facilitate the What is a Campaign? exercise

▷ Lead the Getting Your Voice Heard exercise

▷ Plan and facilitate a discussion about why it's important for young people to get involved in campaigns

▷ Design some statements for and lead the Have YOUR say exercise

▷ Plan and facilitate a discussion based around a campaign film

▷ Research facts and information about young people's involvement in campaigns and where they have made a difference. Plan and lead a session on this

▷ Organise for a speaker from a campaign group to deliver a workshop and chair the workshop

2. PLANNING A CAMPAIGN

Bronze YAA Challenge/ Youth Challenge activities

Take part in activities to explore what makes a good campaign and understand how to plan one.

Possible targets:

- Make a list of all the issues that concern you about your community / the things that affect your life
- Take part in the defining the issue exercise
- Talk to other young people about how they feel about your campaign issue and record their views
- Take part in a quiz on how to plan a good campaign
- Take part in the choosing a campaign goal exercise
- Take part in an activity taking pictures of your local community and using these as evidence to support your campaign arguments
- Take part in the steps to the future exercise
- Take part in an activity to research arguments for and against your campaign issue
- Take part in the choosing your target exercise
- Take part in some research to find out who makes the decisions that affect your campaign.
- Take part in the deciding on your message exercise
- Take part in some research to find out about slogans used by other campaigns
- Take part in the what makes a good slogan exercise
- Take part in the £5 note exercise
- Take part in the lobbying exercise
- Take part in the balloon exercise
- Take part in the Planning a Campaign exercise

- Join in a discussion about the different methods people can use to campaign
- Take part in a discussion about how you will know if your campaign has been successful

Silver YAA Challenge / Youth Challenge Extra

Help run and organise activities for young people to explore what makes a good campaign and understand how to plan one.

Possible targets:

- Help facilitate the Planning a Campaign session
- Help facilitate the Getting Your Voice Heard exercise
- Help plan and lead a discussion about what young people can get from their involvement in campaigns
- Help facilitate the Have YOUR say exercise
- Interview young people about the issues that concern them about their community / the things that affect their lives
- Help run a quiz about how to plan a good campaign
- Co-run the defining the issue exercise
- Work with other young people to support them in the choosing a campaign goal exercise
- Work with other young people to compile photographic evidence of their local community to back up their campaign
- Help facilitate the steps to the future exercise
- Work with other young people to research arguments for and against your campaign issue
- Co-run the choosing your target exercise

Challenges & Targets

CHALLENGES & TARGETS

Possible targets continued:

▷ Work with other young people to research who makes the decisions that affect the campaign

▷ Help facilitate the deciding on your message exercise

▷ Help other young people with research on effective campaign messages

▷ Co-facilitate the what makes a good slogan exercise

▷ Co-facilitate the £5 note exercise

▷ Help run the lobbying exercise

▷ Write a letter to a local decision-maker

▷ Co-facilitate the balloon exercise

▷ Assist with compiling a list of different methods you can use as part of your campaign

▷ Help run the Planning a Campaign session

▷ Assist with research into different ways you can measure the success of your campaign

Gold YAA Challenge

Lead activities for young people to explore what makes a good campaign and understand how to plan one.

Possible targets:

▷ Facilitate the Planning a Campaign exercise

▷ Lead the Getting Your Voice Heard exercise

▷ Plan and facilitate a discussion about what young people can get from their involvement in campaigns

▷ Plan and lead the defining the issue exercise

▷ Facilitate the campaign goal exercise

▷ Research and design a quiz on how to plan a good campaign

▷ Run the steps to the future exercise

▷ Facilitate the choosing your target exercise

▷ Produce a guide / chart for young people illustrating who has the power to make the decisions that affect their campaign

▷ Plan and lead the deciding on your message exercise

▷ Compile a file of case studies of successful campaign messages

▷ Lead the what makes a good slogan exercise

▷ Plan and lead the £5 note exercise

▷ Plan and run the lobbying exercise

▷ Organise a letter-writing campaign to a relevant decision maker

▷ Arrange a meeting with a decision-maker

▷ Lead the balloon exercise

▷ Design some case studies on how to choose the appropriate campaign methods and plan and deliver a session with young people using these case studies.

▷ Research and compile a folder of evidence to support your campaign aim and objectives

▷ Produce a guide on the most useful websites young people can use to research arguments for and against their campaign

▷ Design a series of evaluation exercises to help measure the progress of the campaigninstead and make the debate between them and the campaign

ukyouth Hearing Unheard Voices

3. DOING IT

Bronze YAA Challenge / Youth Challenge activities

Take part in activities that will help young people deliver their campaign.

Possible targets:

- Take part in the team building exercise
- Take part in a discussion about why you want to get involved in the campaign
- Take part in the what I want to achieve exercise
- Take part in a discussion about what you can bring to the campaign and what support you might need to get the most out of it
- Take part in a workshop to design a leaflet / poster
- Hand out leaflets / posters
- Help get people to fill out surveys
- Take part in a photo opportunity
- Take part in a day of action
- Take photographs of your community / what it is you want to change
- Attend a song writing / poetry workshop
- Take part in a drama workshop to explore your campaign issue
- Help out on a stall at a conference to promote your campaign
- Encourage people to sign a petition backing your campaign
- Learn how to set up a campaign Facebook page
- Take part in the how to create an online survey exercise
- Learn about what a blog is
- Take part in a demonstration / protest as part of your campaign
- Take part in session to learn how to set a petition on Number 10 website
- Join a relevant club at school / college
- Attend a public meeting
- Take part in the negotiating skills exercise
- Take part in a workshop learning about how to lobby people in power

CHALLENGES & TARGETS

Silver YAA Challenge / Youth Challenge Extra

Help organise activities that will support young people to deliver their campaign.

Possible targets:

- Help organise the team building exercise
- Help lead a discussion about why young people want to get involved in the campaign
- Support other young people to take part in the what I want to achieve exercise
- Help facilitate a discussion about what young people can bring to the campaign and what support they might need to get the most out of it
- Help plan a workshop to design a leaflet / poster
- Help organise a rota for young people to hand out leaflets / posters
- Help design a survey for young people to use
- Help set up a photo opportunity
- Help plan a day of action
- Work with other young people to take photographs of your community / what it is you want to change
- Help plan and co-facilitate a song writing / poetry workshop
- Help plan a drama workshop to explore the campaign issue in a safe way
- Organise a stall at a conference to promote your campaign
- Set up an online petition backing your campaign
- Work with other young people to set up a Facebook cause and recruit 20 members
- Help to design an online survey
- Work with other young people to set up a campaign blog
- Help set up a relevant club / society at school or college
- Help plan a demonstration / protest as part of your campaign
- Help to facilitate the negotiating exercise
- Help to organise a public meeting, including inviting key decision makers
- Help to plan and lead a workshop learning about how to lobby people in power
- Write a letter to your local councillor / MP

Gold YAA Challenge

Organise and lead activities for young people to enable them to run their campaign.

Possible targets:

- Plan a series of team-building activities to support young people to work better together as a group
- Plan and lead a discussion about why young people want to get involved in the campaign
- Lead the I want to achieve exercise
- Plan and lead a discussion about what young people can bring to the campaign and what support they might need to get the most out of it
- Plan and lead a workshop to design a leaflet / poster
- Design a survey for young people to use
- Liaise with local / national media to set up a photo opportunity
- Organise a day of action in your local community / college
- Plan and lead a project with other young people to collect photographic / video evidence as part of your campaign
- Plan and facilitate a song writing / poetry workshop
- Organise a drama workshop to explore the campaign issue in a safe way
- Set up and run a stall at a conference to promote your campaign
- Design and promote a petition backing your campaign
- Set up and manage a campaign Facebook / web page
- Design, promote and collate an online survey
- Manage a campaign blog
- Set up and run a relevant club or society at your school / college
- Plan and organise a demonstration / protest as part of your campaign, including researching what the legal situation is, approaching the appropriate authorities and negotiating with them.
- Plan and lead the negotiating exercise.
- Plan and organise a public meeting.
- Research, plan and lead a workshop on how to lobby people in power
- Organise a letter writing campaign to your local councillors / MPGold YAA Challenge

CHALLENGES & TARGETS

4. SHOUT ABOUT IT!

Bronze YAA Challenge / Youth Challenge activities

Take part in activities to learn about publicising your campaign.

Possible targets:

- Take part in a discussion about how young people are represented in the media
- Talk to other young people about how they think they are represented in the media
- Take part in a research exercise to find out how young people are represented – collect newspaper, magazine articles, look at newspaper websites, the BBC etc.
- Take part in the exercise on dealing with the media
- Attend a workshop on presentation skills
- Attend a talk by someone involved in your campaign
- Take part in a discussion about the pros and cons of involving celebrities in your campaign
- Take part in an exercise to decide who you could approach to back your campaign
- Take part in a letter-writing exercise to a celebrity

Silver Challenge / Youth Challenge Extra Activities

Help organise and run activities about publicising your campaign.

Possible targets:

- Help plan and facilitate a discussion about how young people are represented in the media
- Help design a survey to find out how other young people think they are represented in the media
- Compile an evidence file on how young people are represented – collect newspaper, magazine articles, look at newspaper websites, the BBC etc.
- Help to lead on the exercise on dealing with the media
- Help to plan a workshop on presentation skills
- Plan a talk on your campaign issue
- Help plan and facilitate a discussion about the pros and cons of involving celebrities in your campaign
- Help to design an exercise to decide who you could approach to back your campaign
- Help lead a letter-writing exercise to a celebrity

Gold YAA Challenge

Organise and run activities to support young people to publicise their campaign.

Possible targets:

- Plan and lead a discussion about how young people are represented in the media
- Research, design and co-ordinate a survey to find out how other young people think they are represented in the media
- Collect evidence on how young people are represented in the media and use it to design a quiz / some case studies for use with other young people
- Plan and lead the exercise on dealing with the media
- Plan and lead a workshop on presentation skills
- Research, plan and deliver a presentation on your campaign issue
- Research and lead a discussion about the pros and cons of involving celebrities in your campaign
- Collect examples of celebrities who are associated with campaigns and lead a discussion on how well these have worked
- Design and run an exercise to decide who you could approach to back your campaign
- Run a letter-writing exercise to a celebrity with other young people

ACCREDITATION

UK YOUTH'S CHALLENGES AND YOUTH ACHIEVEMENT AWARDS

The Youth Challenges and Youth Achievement Awards (The Awards) are a flexible framework for accrediting the engagement and learning of children and young people generally aged between 11 and 25.

The Youth Achievement Awards (YAA) were launched in 1997, the Youth Challenges (YC) in 2002, and building on the success of these, UK Youth launched the Junior Achievement Award in 2008 to meet the demand for an award for under 11s. Initially established specifically for use in non-formal education settings, the awards are now increasingly being used by schools, colleges and training providers to motivate and engage their young people.

The Awards are an activity-based approach to peer education and are designed to help develop more effective participative practice by encouraging young people to take increasing responsibility for their lives and learning, and to develop the personal and social skills that will benefit them in all aspects of life and employment.

They are designed to:

- Recognise and accredit young people's achievements
- Encourage young people to become more involved in developing their own programmes based on their interests
- Promote young people's participation in decision making and ownership of their activities and learning
- Motivate young people by giving them a sense of achievement and recognition
- Lead to identifiable skills development

They enable young people to:

- Enhance self-awareness and self-esteem
- Develop communication skills and resolve differences by negotiation
- Get on with and work well with others
- Explore and manage feelings
- Understand and identify with others
- Develop values
- Plan ahead

The Awards are accessible to all young people regardless of academic achievement, and, in particular, are an effective tool to engage young people who are at risk of social exclusion.

They are a peer assessed, portfolio based learning framework for young people that is accredited to national standards by ASDAN – an awarding body recognised by the Qualifications and Curriculum Authority (QCA). In Scotland, the Awards are credit rated by the Scottish Credit and Qualifications Framework.

ACCREDITATION

Levels

The Awards are based upon the youth work Curriculum Development Model, a way of working whereby the young person (supported and guided by the worker) progressively takes on responsibility for their own involvement, their learning and their actions.

There are 4 levels of responsibility that can be recognised through the Youth Achievement Award and 2 levels through the Youth Challenges:

- Bronze YAA / Youth Challenges: taking part in activities
- Silver YAA / Youth Challenge Extra: helping run and organise activities
- Gold YAA: planning, organising and leading activities
- Platinum YAA: leading other young people (peer leadership)

Young people should enter the Awards at the level most appropriate to their interests and abilities. For example, young people who are taking part in activities would undertake Bronze YAA or the Youth Challenge. Young people who are helping run and organise activities would undertake Silver YAA or the Youth Challenge Extra.

It is possible for activities and challenges at different levels to be running concurrently within a group and there are examples of this in the Sample Activities and Challenges listed in this toolkit. For example, a young person doing a Gold Challenge may research and design a quiz on how to plan a good campaign as one of their targets. Young people doing a Bronze Challenge may then take part in the quiz as one of their targets.

Youth Achievement Awards
Curriculum Development Model

Youth Challenges	Youth Achievement Awards		Levels of Responsilbility
	Platinum	▷ Leadership or peer education role	**Stage 5:** Lead
	Gold	▷ Plan, organise and lead activities	**Stage 6:** Organise
YC Extra	Silver	▷ Help to organise activities	**Stage 5:** Be Involved
YC	Bronze	▷ Take part in activities	**Stage 4:** Take Part
		▷ Engage in regular discussions	**Stage 3:** Socialise
		▷ Meet regularly	**Stage 2:** Meet Again
		▷ Make initial contact	**Stage 1:** Contact

A progressive model of youth worker involvement with young people

(after Gloucestershire Youth and Community Service) © John Huskins

ACCREDITATION

How long do the Awards take to complete?

Youth Challenge / Youth Challenge Extra
This takes 30 hours to achieve, divided into 5 x 6 hours of activity.

Bronze Youth Achievement Award
This takes 60 hours to achieve, divided into 4 x 15 hour activities, called challenges.

Silver Youth Achievement Award
This takes 90 hours to achieve, divided into 6 x 15 hour challenges.

Gold Youth Achievement Award
This requires the young person to complete seven 15 hour challenges and make a presentation.

Young people can accrue the hours they need over days, weeks or months, and ideally these should be logged in a timesheet.

Platinum Youth Achievement Award
This award is structured slightly differently and takes approximately 120 hours to complete. It can be completed over several months or longer, but should be done within 2 years. The Platinum Award requires young people to go through a process of developing the skills they will need to undertake the role of peer leader and for this reason young people need to be at least 16 years old when they start the Award.

The Platinum Award requires young people to:

- Produce a personal development plan
- Take part in training (approximately 30 hours equivalent)
- Undertake a placement involving working with and leading other young people (approximately 60 hours equivalent)
- Evaluate their progress
- Prepare and deliver a presentation

This toolkit can be used as resource for young people who act as peer leaders, such as volunteer youth workers, or peer educators, in their planning and delivery of campaigning activities.

The Structure of the Awards

Youth Challenges 6 Hour Activities	
Youth Challenge 30 Hours	**Youth Challenge Extra** 30 Hours
Activity 1	Activity 1
Activity 2	Activity 2
Activity 3	Activity 3
Activity 4	Activity 4
Activity 5	Activity 5

Youth Achievement Awards 15 Hour Activities			Variable Activities
Bronze 60 Hours	**Silver** 90 Hours	**Gold** 120 Hours	**Platinum** 120 Hours
Challenge 1	Challenge 1	Challenge 1	Challenge 1 *Personal Development Plan*
Challenge 2	Challenge 2	Challenge 2	Challenge 2 *Training (min 30 hours)*
Challenge 3	Challenge 3	Challenge 3	
Challenge 4	Challenge 4	Challenge 4	Challenge 3 *Work Placement (min 60 hours)*
	Challenge 5	Challenge 5	
	Challenge 6	Challenge 6	
		Challenge 7	
		Challenge 8 *Presentation*	Challenge 4 *Evaluation*
			Challenge 4 *Presentation*

Accreditation

ACCREDITATION

Progression within the Awards

Young people can progress through the Awards, gaining credits that count towards the next level of Award, up to the Gold Youth Achievement Award. The Awards can also count towards various ASDAN awards and qualifications.

Flexibility of Awards

The Awards are very flexible. There is no prescribed programme of activities; young people choose what it is they want to do, based on what the organisation is able to support. For the Youth Achievement Awards, young people set themselves a number of clear and achievable targets, between 2 and 4 per challenge. By setting their own targets young people develop a sense of ownership and increased motivation to undertake the challenges.

What is a challenge?

A challenge is an activity that the young person intends to do and which is either new to that young person or builds upon their previous achievements. All of the Awards are broken down into a series of challenges (called activities when doing the Youth Challenges).

Challenges should be based on the interests and concerns of the young people themselves. It is important to remember that what is a "challenge" to one young person may not be a challenge to another.

Top Tip When recording the planned challenges, the young person should try to give a full description of the activity. For example, *"to take part in a residential weekend with my youth group"* gives far more information than simply saying *"residential"*.

What is a Target?

The challenges are made more accessible by further dividing them into targets. Targets are what the young person plans to achieve when doing their challenge. The targets might be a series of steps in the process needed to complete a challenge, or they might identify particular individual goals that the young person wants to achieve.

Targets should be tailored to meet the needs of each individual young person. For example, there may be a whole group who plan to "Attend a residential event" as a shared challenge, but within that, each young person should pinpoint what they, as an individual, aim to achieve during the challenge.

Top Tip The most interesting challenges use targets which are not only skills and knowledge based (e.g. "learn how to plan a presentation", "find out who the key decision makers are in my area"), but also include attitudinal based targets, such as "improve my self confidence when talking in front of a group" or "learn to work better as part of a team".

Be SMART

When planning their challenges, young people should be encouraged to check that their challenges and targets are "SMART":

S – specific: Does the young person know exactly what the challenge involves?

M – measurable: How will the young person know when they have achieved their target?

A – achievable: Can the target be achieved using the resources available?

R – realistic: How likely is it that the young person will be able to complete the challenge? Consider their track record for completing things and make sure they are not setting themselves up to fail.

T – timebound: How long will the target take to be completed and how will the young person know when it is completed? For example, "getting on well with the group" is not timebound, but "getting on well with the group during the residential" is.

Recording the Process

Young people need to record and review their challenges, which they do in their Award booklet (called Challenge booklets when doing the Youth Challenges). The booklets contain all the key questions that must be answered in order to complete the Awards.

In addition, each young person undertaking the Awards must produce a portfolio of evidence demonstrating what they have achieved, and showing how they have met their targets while completing their challenges. Ideally, the activities themselves will naturally generate evidence for portfolios.

Presenting Portfolio Evidence

- Portfolios should be as well organised as possible – for example, it is helpful for evidence relating to individual challenges to be clearly separated

- As evidence for length of time spent on challenges, it can be useful to break down some of the elements – for example, include simple timesheets, diaries or logs

- Remember it's about quality of evidence, not quantity. Quality evidence should demonstrate with certainty that each individual target has been worked towards

- Visual evidence, such as photographs, pictures, drawings, illustrations or objects should be given some explanation (e.g. captions) to show why they have been included and how they relate to the challenge

- Portfolio evidence should clearly reflect the experience and learning of the individual young person. Pre-prepared handouts, leaflets, group photos, DVDs, photocopied or downloaded documents are all acceptable evidence but need to be personalised by the young person using notes, Post-it notes, handwritten comments or some other means of explaining the relevance of this evidence to the individual young person

- Literacy skills are not a requirement for the Youth Achievement Award. As long as the evidence can be attributed to the young person (by counter signature or witness statement, for example) it will be acceptable

> **Top Tip**
>
> The portfolio must demonstrate that the individual young person:
>
> - Was involved in the activity
> - Worked towards their targets
> - Took the appropriate amount of responsibility according to the level of Award that they are completing
> - Spent the minimum amount of time needed on each challenge
> - Completed the appropriate number of challenges
>
> UK Youth offer training on effective portfolio building.

Delivering the Youth Achievement Awards

To deliver the Awards to young people, workers will need to take part in a UK Youth YAA Introductory Training day and organisations will need to register to deliver the Awards. Further information on this can be found on the UK Youth website **www.ukyouth.org.uk** and the YAA website **www.youthachievementawards.org** or by e-mailing **yaa@ukyouth.org**

The Youth Challenges and Youth Achievement Awards are externally accredited by ASDAN. For more information about ASDAN visit **www.asdan.co.uk**

Examples of Portfolio Evidence

Evidence that shows that the young person:	Produced by the young person	Collected by the young person	Produced by others
Was involved in the activity	▷ Photographs ▷ Video recording ▷ Tape recording ▷ Statements ▷ Drawings ▷ Questionnaires ▷ Letters ▷ E-mails ▷ Phone records ▷ Plans ▷ Designs ▷ Posters ▷ Memos ▷ Notices ▷ Posters ▷ Diary ▷ Scripts	▷ Consent forms ▷ Receipts ▷ Leaflets ▷ Booklets ▷ Travel tickets ▷ Events tickets ▷ Flyers ▷ Maps ▷ Course notes ▷ Research ▷ Newspaper cuttings ▷ Certificates	▷ Youth worker / teacher observations ▷ Witness observations ▷ Employer observations ▷ Family observations ▷ Peer observations
Worked towards their targets	▷ Questionnaires ▷ Review forms ▷ Evaluation forms ▷ Feedback sessions ▷ Diary ▷ Log book ▷ Timelines	▷ Certificates ▷ Test results	▷ Witness observations ▷ Peer observations ▷ Attendance records
Took the appropriate amount of responsibility	▷ Role descriptions ▷ Work plans ▷ Task sheets ▷ Diary ▷ Log book	▷ Minutes of meetings	▷ Witness observations ▷ Attendance records
Spent the minimum time needed on each challenge	▷ Diary ▷ Log book ▷ Time sheet	▷ Records of attendance ▷ Signing in sheets	▷ Witness statements ▷ Attendance records
Completed the appropriate number of challenges	▷ Award booklet	▷ Challenge certificates	▷ Witness statements

ACCREDITATION

Using the Youth Challenges and Youth Achievement Awards in a Formal Education Setting

Although the Youth Challenges and Youth Achievement Awards were originally created for use in non-formal education settings, they are increasingly being taken up by schools and colleges. The issue of campaigning and the skills and abilities young people can acquire through their involvement with campaigns complement areas for learning at Key Stages 3 and 4, particularly in the subject areas of citizenship and PSHE.

Citizenship: ages 11-14

Key stage 3.

Participating and taking action

During key stage 3, pupils follow the compulsory programme of study for citizenship. They learn about their rights and responsibilities, duties and freedoms, laws and justice, and democratic institutions, parliament and government.

As part of the national curriculum for citizenship at key stage 3, pupils:

- research, analyse and reflect on a wide range of controversial issues
- take part in different kinds of discussions and debates
- participate in different forms of individual and collective action
- work with a range of voluntary and public organisations and the local council
- use different media and ICT to interpret and communicate ideas
- learn techniques to persuade others and represent different points of view.

Citizenship: ages 14-16

Key stage 4

Tackling real issues

During key stage 4, pupils follow the compulsory programme of study for citizenship, which builds on what they learnt at key stage 3. They learn more about their rights and responsibilities, duties and freedoms, laws and justice and democratic institutions. They learn about different forms of government, both democratic and non-democratic, and consider the challenges facing the global community, including international disagreements and conflict, global inequalities, sustainability and the use of the world's resources.

PSHE

The personal wellbeing programme of study provides opportunities to plan sequences of work, learning outcomes and teaching approaches that develop:

- Successful learners
- Confident individuals
- Responsible citizens

For further information go to **www.qcda.gov.uk.**

Citizenship in Scotland

The Scottish approach to education for citizenship differs from others areas of the United Kingdom, because it has not introduced a specific subject called 'Citizenship'. Instead, all subjects are expected to make their relevance to education for citizenship explicit, and that the issues associated with citizenship will be developed through whole-school and cross-curricular activities.

For further information go to **www.ltscotland.org.uk/citizenship**

Links to Other Awards and Qualifications

The flexible framework of the Awards enables cross-accreditation with a whole range of other awards and qualifications so young people gain a Youth Achievement Award in addition to their other award / qualification. For example, young people can gain YAA Challenges while working towards their Duke of Edinburgh Award.

Additional Information

ACCREDITATION

GCSE Citizenship Studies

Involvement in a campaign challenge can support students working towards a GCSE in Citizenship Studies, where they are required to tackle real issues as part of an active citizenship project.

Act by Right

Act by Right is an accredited training programme to support young people in developing the skills for making change happen.

Act by Right has five units. Each unit has three aims and each aim has three activities. It takes about three hours to complete each aim. With the hour review of learning at the end of each unit, it takes ten hours to complete each unit. You can also use *Act by Right* towards certification by ASDAN.

The five units are:

1. Getting to know each other and representing others

Aims:

- Understanding each other
- Appreciating and respecting other people
- Representing other people

2. Getting to know our community

Aims:

- Understanding communities
- Mapping communities
- Identifying community links and support

3. Getting ready for action

Aims:

- Agreeing the group's priority for action
- Developing an action plan for change
- Building alliances

4. Campaigning for change

Aims:

- Creating a clear message
- Getting the message across
- Keeping the campaign alive

5. Finding out what's changed

Aims:

- Understanding about evaluation
- Tooling up for evaluation
- Doing the evaluation

All the review sheets for each unit and a number of the activities have activity sheets you can photocopy and use.

For more information on Act By Right go to: www.hbr.nya.org.uk/

QCDA Personal and Social Development Units

These units offer ways of supporting young people in the following:

- Becoming confident individuals who are physically, emotionally and socially healthy
- Being responsible citizens who make a positive contribution to society and embrace change

The PSD Units can be undertaken by 14-19 year olds as well as adults, and can be gained in schools, colleges and the non-formal education sector. They are on the Qualifications and Credit Framework and can be accessed through a range of awarding bodies. Further information can be found at **www.qca.gov.uk**

ADDITIONAL INFORMATION

This section contains some supplementary information on a number of aspects of campaigning.

Contents

Campaigning in Context

Data Protection

Contacting politicians

Lobbying Local Government

Lobbying MPs

Public Protests and the Law

The Campaigner's Dictionary

Where to go for further support

CAMPAIGNING IN CONTEXT

Recent years have seen considerable policy development and transformation in the areas of children's services in England and Wales. This rapidly changing context has promoted a new vision for children and young people, with an increasing emphasis being placed on providing opportunities for children and young people to make a positive contribution to the communities in which they reside.

Every Child Matters

Every Child Matters and the Children Act 2004 create the foundation for the government's Change for Children programme. The government's aim is for every child, whatever their background or their circumstances, to have the support they need to:

- Be healthy
- Stay safe
- Enjoy and achieve
- Make a positive contribution
- Achieve economic well being.

http://www.everychildmatters.gov.uk

Youth Matters

Youth Matters is a continuation of the work begun in Every Child Matters, and focuses on improving outcomes for 13-19 year olds. It aims to develop a strategy to provide young people with opportunities, challenges and support and proposes that young people should have:

- More things to do and places to go in their local area – and more choice and influence over what is available
- More opportunities to volunteer and to make a contribution to their local community
- Better information, advice and guidance about issues that matter to them, delivered in the way they want to receive it

Through the reforms identified in Youth Matters, the government wants to see a radical reshaping of services for all teenagers and part if the idea is to empower young people to shape their local services, involve them in local decision making and provide opportunities for them to give something back to their communities.

http://www.everychildmatters.gov.uk/youthmatters

Additional Information

ADDITIONAL INFORMATION

DATA PROTECTION

As part of your campaign, you're going to need to recruit supporters, which means at some point you're probably going to have to collect their personal details (phone numbers, e-mail addresses etc), so that you can keep them posted on what you're up to.

What you'll need to remember in that case, is that you have a responsibility not to misuse this private information.

If you have asked someone to sign a petition to support your cause, you can't then sell their details on to a market research company!

You also have a responsibility to keep this information safe.

As long as you tell people what you are going to do with their details and stick to it, you should be ok.

For more information on data protection, you can check out the Information Commissioner's Office at **http://www.ico.gov.uk/**

CONTACTING POLITICIANS

Local politicians

You can find out who your local councillor or Mayor is on the internet by going to your local authority website, or by phoning your local Town Hall. The number for the Town Hall will be in your local telephone directory and the yellow pages.

Contacting your MP

To find out who your MP is you can go on the internet and look up **www.theyworkforyou.com** or go to your local authority website. You can also call the House of Commons Information Office on **020 7219 4272** or your local Town Hall.

Contacting your MEP

Your MEP (Member of European Parliament) might be a useful person to contact, particularly if your campaign is related to an issue like the environment. You can go direct to the European Parliament website for details **http://www.europarl.org.uk/section/your-meps/your-meps** or you an easier way might be to enter your postcode into **http://www.writetothem.com/** – this will tell you who your local MEP is, and actually your local Councillors and MPs too!

Writing to Politicians

All local councillors will have an address at the local Town Hall for you to write to. All MPs have Westminster offices or have arrangements for their mail to be dealt with or redirected when they are away from London, so it's better to write to them at the House of Commons, rather than to their constituency office or home address.

The address to write to is: Name of MP, House of Commons, London SW1A 0AA.

Additional Information

ADDITIONAL INFORMATION

LOBBYING LOCAL GOVERNMENT[1]

Local authorities, or councils as they are more commonly known, will often be a key target of campaigns.

Even if your campaign goes beyond a local area, getting your local council on board could be the best way to make an impact. And it's not just about lobbying your local councillor either.

Officers

Start off by talking to staff at the local council who are working on issues related to what you are campaigning on. They are not elected and not political.

To find out who the right officer to contact is, you could try writing to the head of the relevant department or Chief Executive and ask for the enquiry to be referred to the right person. Alternatively, you could try phoning the council to find out who you need to contact.

If you are campaigning on an issue that the local authority is already actively involved in, find out if and when any decisions will be made, then find out who will be responsible for making the decision.

You will also need to find out how that decision will be made. Will there be a public consultation on the issue, or is it something that will be discussed at a council meeting, and if so, how can you get your views represented at that meeting?

Once a decision has been made, is it final or is there a chance to appeal if it goes against what you're asking for?

Write to the relevant officer and be clear about your views, present them with any facts you have, any local consultation you've undertaken, and provide an alternative scenario or solution to the one proposed.

If you do this well, rather than being seen as an opponent, the relevant officer may actually want to find out more about your views and even invite you on to relevant advisory committees.

On things like policy matters, it is unlikely that an officer will be in a position to affect change, as that will be a decision for councillors to make. However, the officer can still be important, as councillors may well ask the officer to make a recommendation to them.

Councillors

While many officers' recommendations are accepted by council committees, it can be hard to predict what way things will go. So you should ensure that you follow the issue as it passes through the council.

A local authority will usually be controlled by one political party or group, which holds a majority of seats on the council. The leader of that group then becomes the leader of the council (not the same as the local MP). The political power in the council sits in the leader's office.

In 'hung councils', where no party has an overall majority, the leadership would actually be shared. In some cases, parties may form a coalition to achieve a majority. However hung councils operate, lobbyists need to be aware of each of the parties' interests.

Theoretically at least, a hung council is good for lobbyists (as it is for small parties), in that it increases their potential to effectively lobby.

In summary, if your campaign is targeting a local council, do some research so that you understand where the power lies.

MPs and Local Councils

The Member of Parliament (MP) for a constituency actually does not have any formal power over the local council. However, they can be an effective voice to the council on your behalf. They can be especially useful in helping you to achieve press coverage.

If you are making a complaint about a local council, an MPs' involvement could mean it is handled with greater care. MPs also raise issues in Parliament that affect their constituents e.g. by putting questions to ministers with relevant responsibilities. This will in turn have an effect at the local council level, as the Minister will probably ask a departmental civil servant to get more information from your council!

Don't forget about prospective parliamentary candidates too. To nurture a relationship with parliamentarians can take time, and so you do need to look beyond who has influence now, to who might have influence in 12 months.

[1] Information taken from "The Campaigning Handbook" – Mark Lattimer

LOBBYING MPS

Finding Your Way Around the House of Commons

The House of Commons has 646 MPs, all of whom represent a specific constituency (area) in England, Wales, Scotland or Northern Ireland. Then there are the government departments, which are headed by the various ministers and staffed by civil servants: these departments are watched over by select committees. There are also public bill committees, and there are joint committees that work with the House of Lords. All of these are possible points of entry for campaigners looking for suitable people to lobby. There are similar opportunities to be found at the Welsh Assembly, the Northern Ireland Assembly and the Scottish Parliament.

Find out more about your MP

Whether your MP is a Minister, a backbencher or in opposition will affect how they vote in Parliament. A backbench MP will have a lot more freedom than a Minister about how they vote. A Minister is expected to be consistently loyal to the government. MPs get an indication of how they are supposed to vote by their "Party Whip" and they will normally vote with their own party. They may rebel and vote with the opposition if they feel particularly strongly about an issue.

Sometimes the government will declare a "free vote" and this means that all MPs can vote according to their own conscience. This is what happened with the fox hunting bill.

You can find out about your MPs interests, what they say and how they vote on any issue from **www.theyworkforyou.com**

As well as helping you to find out who your MPs, you can also use this site to:

- Search House of Commons and House of Lords debates, written answers and statements for an MP, constituency or debate
- Sign up to be e-mailed whenever your MP speaks

It can also help you to find out whether your MP is already aware of your issue, whether they have made speeches, asked questions or which way they voted if they had to vote.

If you want to see if your MP belongs to a special interest group called an "All Party Parliamentary Group" (APPG), then you need to look at the official Parliament website. This can be found at **www.parliament.uk** These groups have a voluntary membership.

All Parliamentary Groups (APPG)

Parliament has a number of groups concerned with a wide variety of subject. Membership of these groups is drawn from backbench members of all political parties in the House and they provide an opportunity for cross-party discussion and co-operation on particular issues. All-party groups sometimes act as useful pressure groups for specific causes helping to keep the government, the opposition and MPs informed of parliamentary and outside opinion. The range of subjects they cover is large and includes things like animal welfare, sport, the environment, science and civil liberties.

How MPs can influence on your behalf

There are a number of ways that an MP may be able to help you. They can provide advice or write letters on your behalf to officials or Ministers. If appropriate, your MP can choose to raise your case in the House of Commons through a parliamentary question, in an adjournment debate or in an early day motion.

See over for a list of things your MP can do to help you get information and answers or to influence and create change:

ADDITIONAL INFORMATION

Parliamentary Questions

Parliamentary questions are used by Members of Parliament to seek information or press for action. All questions, whether written or spoken, are recorded in The Official Report (Hansard) and so they are widely available and accessible.

The purpose is to get an answer "on the record", so you get evidence relevant to your issue. There is a real knack to getting the phrasing of these correct in order to get the answer you need and this is where your MP can help. You should also be aware that there is also a real knack to avoiding giving the answer you want to hear!

Adjournment Debates

These are also called Westminster Hall Debates. An adjournment debate is a short half hour debate which is introduced by a backbencher at the end of each day's business in the House of Commons. It gives backbench members the opportunity to discuss issues of concern to them and to have a minister to respond to the points they raise. A weekly ballot decides which backbench members will get to choose the subject for each daily debate. Backbenchers normally use this as an opportunity to debate issues related to their constituency.

Early Day Motion

An Early Day Motion (EDM) is an MPs equivalent of a petition. The modern-day purpose of EDMs is to allow MPs to express their opinion on a subject and to canvass support for their views by inviting other members to add their signatures in support of the statement.

Private Members' Bills

Early in the new session of Parliament there is a ballot amongst MPs to introduce a private members' bill. Usually only the first few chosen will stand any chance of their bill becoming law. This process allows time on the floor of the House of Commons to debate short, specific issues.

Ten Minute Rule Bills

These offer an opportunity for MPs to speak for ten minutes on a specific issue. They are a good opportunity for publicity because the speaking slots occur just after Question Time in the House of Commons and before the main afternoon debate when journalists are still present. These bills never get anywhere but are a good opportunity to highlight a particular issue.

PUBLIC PROTESTS AND THE LAW

Slightly different laws apply to demonstrations (static protests on public land) and processions/marches along a planned route.

Demonstrations

If you're planning a demonstration, you're free to do it pretty much anywhere, so long as it's not within the "designated area" around parliament in which case you will need to have police permission.

You're not allowed to obstruct the highway, any road or path that the public are allowed to pass on, as this is a criminal offence under the Highways Act 1980.

You also need to remain polite and not threatening, otherwise you could be accused of aggravated trespass under the Criminal Justice and Public Order Act 1994.

If you have more than five vehicles, under the same act, the police can ask you to leave. However, it is quite possible that if you are protesting peacefully and causing absolutely no disruption you will be left completely alone.

If you are planning to enter a building, then the situation changes somewhat. If you need to use force in any way to enter the building, then you may be guilty of aggravated trespass or criminal damage. If however you enter in a peaceful way, do not harass anyone and remain polite throughout, then you are only committing a civil offence, so the police, strictly speaking, should not get involved. Although they may still be called in and may still carry you out of there, they are very unlikely to charge you: it would be up to the owners of the buildings to prosecute you privately. And that happens very very rarely.

Marches

If you are organising a march, you need to begin by letting the police know. You will need to give them the names and contact details of the organisers, as well as the date and time and the proposed route – and you should get this to them a week before the march is to take place.

If that's not possible, then do it by hand as soon as is reasonably possible. If it is a truly spontaneous march, then you may be exempt.

The police have the power to impose conditions on a march, or even to stop it from happening, but it may be worth reminding them that you can dispute their decision through the courts. They must show that they believe the march may result in serious public disorder, serious damage to property or serious disruption to the life of the community, or that the organisers' purpose is "the intimidation of others with a view to compelling them not to do an act they have a right to do, or do an act they have a right not to do".

If you fail to comply with police conditions, you could face up to 51 weeks in prison. And anyone who even goes on a march that has been banned – let alone continues to organise it – could also go down for 51 weeks.

Banners, posters, placards and leaflets...

These can get you into trouble if the wording isn't right. The Public Order Act 1986 bans the display of material that could be threatening, abusive or insulting to members of the public, or provoke violence, or cause members of the public to fear violence, or cause harassment, alarm or distress.

You're also not allowed to "solicit" murder, so best to avoid calling for the annihilation of anyone!

ADDITIONAL INFORMATION

THE CAMPAIGNER'S DICTIONARY

Action Committee – An organisation set up in the interest of achieving something specific for a campaign group. The action committee typically spreads a message, creates petitions/protest and solicits/collects campaign contributions.

Advisory Group – A group of individuals formed to advise an organisation on a particular subject, their general priorities or on service development. Members are typically chosen based on personal experience and knowledge and should be formed to cover a broad range of social and economic classes. These groups have no formal authority but serve in making recommendations and provide information that will aid the organisation in forming a plan. Advisory groups can be formed and stand for one specific topic or be on going through varies topics/changes in the organisation.

Assembly – A group of people gathered together for a common reason.

London Assembly – Established in 2000 as part of the Greater London Authority, this elected group is in charge of investigating issues important to Londoners, publishing findings and recommendations, making proposals to the Mayor, and has the right to amend the Mayor's annual budget with a two-thirds majority.

Ballot – A method of collecting and recording votes in any given election.

Secret Ballot – A voting method were voter's choices are kept confidential in an effort to stop attempts to influence voters through intimidation or bribery.

BAME – Interest group that represents the political and social interests of Black, Asian and minority ethnics, including mixed ethnics groups such as Asian British, Black, Black British, Chinese, etc

Campaign/Campaigning – A series of co-ordinated activities, such as speeches and petitions, designed in an effort to inform and convince citizens of a particular cause or to influence their political decisions by persuasive techniques.

Campaign Committee – A group of members of the same organisation, fighting for the same cause or for the same person that they want to be elected. A Campaign Committee helps the candidate or issue to gain support.

Campaign Materials – Various products/tactics used to promote a campaign. Materials include, but are not limited to, the following:

Posters/Photographs – Materials intended to be hung up to advertise your campaign and raise awareness of who you are / what you are trying to achieve.

Slogan – A phrase expressing the aim of a campaign; a motto.

Youtube – A video sharing website that gives political participants, interest groups, and organisations the chance to share advertisements, campaign messages, and general information with their supporters as well as the general public.

Facebook – a social networking site often used to gain group support and recruit people for particular causes or campaigns.

Badges/Campaign Buttons – button created with a picture or slogan for your campaign on it for supporters to wear.

Telephoning – A method of reaching supporters by calling them in order to discuss your campaign.

Candidate Statement – A document outlining a candidate's policies, plans and ideas, written in order to inform voters on the stance a candidate holds on issues important to the election and constituency and their intentions once elected.

Canvassing – To go out talking to people to ask for votes or opinions on particular issues that affect your campaign.

Challenge – Youth Achievement Awards are broken down into a series of challenges (called activities when doing the Youth Challenge). A challenge is an activity that the young person intends to do and which is either new to that young person or builds upon their previous achievements.

Constituency – The body of voters/residents in a district represented by an elected official; the district represented by said official.

Consultation – Asking people's views on a particular issue or policy that affects them.

Elected members – People who have been elected to the Council / councillors.

Election – A process where the population decides the individual who will hold an office for the coming term.

UK General Election – Election for the Members of Parliament (MPs) forming the UK House of Commons. According to the Parliament Act 1911 each parliamentary session can last a maximum of five years, ending with dissolution of Parliament.

National/Regional Parliament and Assemblies – Elections for the Members of Scottish Parliament (MSPs), Members of the National Assembly of Wales (AMs), and the Northern Ireland Assembly are held every four years.

European parliament – Every five years elections are held in electoral regions throughout the European Union (EU) in order to elect the Members of the European Parliament (MEPs). The UK has 72 MEPs (down from 78 in the last elections due to the growth of the EU) and 12 electoral regions.

Local Elections – Held every year to elect local councillors. In years with a general election the local elections are traditionally held on the same day as the general.

Empowerment – To give ability, power or authority to someone.

Focus – A centre of action, attention, or campaigning; a point of concentration.

Government – The governing body of a set region or group of individuals that is expected to enforce, protect, and establish laws in order to uphold the body that it governs.

Independent – A politician who is not affiliated with any political party.

Involvement – This is the over-all term for children and young people being included in decision-making. This can range from young people being involved at the suggestion of adults, without having any real understanding of the process, right through to young people being the ones who come up with the ideas and invite adults to join in on their terms.

LGBT – Represents the lesbian, gay, bisexual, and transgender people.

The UK's National LGBT Youth Organisation (Queer Youth Network) – Run by the LGBT, the QYN works towards representing the views of lesbian and gay youth in the UK as well as offering support and information to UK youth facing coming out and homophobia.

Stonewall – A lesbian, gay, and bisexual interest group formed in the UK in 1989 by members of the Labour Party lobbying against Section 28 of the Local Government Act (which stated persons "shall not intentionally promote homosexuality or publish material with the intention of promoting homosexuality" or "promote the teaching in any maintained school of the acceptability of homosexuality as a pretended family relationship"). Today Stonewall works in lobbying and policy development concerning the rights of lesbian, gay, and bisexual community in connection with LGBT.

ADDITIONAL INFORMATION

Lobbying – The ongoing attempt to influence the opinions of leaders and politicians that are active in making decisions. Lobbying is a way of seeking to explain your campaign and its message to those who may be in a position to decide on the issue or influence decisions. Lobbying is a structured approach to getting your campaign and its message across to those people who can help you make a difference.

Mandate – The authority granted to an electorate to represent the constituency and implement certain policies. The period a government serves between elections is also called a mandate while a government seeking re-election is said to be seeking a new mandate.

Manifesto – Please see campaign statement.

Media – A wide array of ways to store and communicate information. Different types of media include, but are not limited to the following:

Mass Media – The flow of information across all means of mass communication.

Broadcast Media – The flow of information across mass electronic communication stations and networks.

Print Media – The flow of information through printed communication means such as newspapers, magazines, books, etc.

News Media – The flow of newsworthy information through various means of communication.

Digital Media – The flow of information maintained by storing, transmitting, and receiving of digitalized information.

Message – Information that is communicated to another person or persons. In campaigning, it is the ideas or points that you want to get across to people.

Opinion Poll – A survey of public opinion on a particular topic or candidate typically given to a random sample of people.

Participation – Actively taking part in and influencing the political and decision-making process.

Pledge – A promise that you have every intention of fulfilling once the election is done. This can include doing something or stopping something.

Political Party – An organisation of people with similar political ideals and opinions who work towards influencing public policy.

Labour Party – Created during the 20th Century, the Labour Party has grown into the major mid-left party in the UK. Gordon Brown, the party leader, is also currently the Prime Minister of the UK. To learn more about the Labour Party please visit http://www.labour.org.uk/.

Conservative Party (Tories) – Created in the early 19th century, the Conservatives have traditionally been regarded as the major right party, though recently they are commonly considered centre-right. For more information please visit www.conservatives.com.

Liberal Democrats – The centre/centre-left party formed in 1988. To learn more about the Liberal Democrats please visit www.libdems.org.uk.

Green – Made up of three separate federal parties – The Green Party of England and Wales, the Green Party of Northern Ireland, and the Scottish Green Party – who work together on varies ecologic campaigns throughout the UK. For more information please visit www.greenparty.org.uk.

Scottish National Party – A centre-left party, which campaigns for Scottish Independence. For more information on this party please visit www.snp.org.

Plaid Cymru – The national party of Wales who campaigns for the creation of Wales as independent state within the European Union. For more information on Plaid Cymru please visit www.plaidcymru.org.

Ulster Conservatives and Unionists – An electoral alliance between the Ulster Unionist Party and the Conservative Party for the 2009 European Parliament election and certain subsequent elections in Northern Ireland. For more information please refer to www.uup.org.

Sinn Fein – The left political party in Northern Ireland that stands for the people. For more information please visit **www.sinnfein.ie.**

Democratic Unionist Party – The larger of the two main unionist political parties in Northern Ireland, currently stands as the largest party in the Northern Ireland Assembly and the fourth-largest party in the House of Commons in the United Kingdom. For more information please visit **http://www.dup.org.uk/.**

United Kingdom Independence Party – Formed in 1993, the UKIP was set up to fight for the withdrawal of the United Kingdom from the European Union. To learn more about UKIP please visit **http://www.ukip.org/.**

British National Party – Formed in 1982, the BNP is a far-right, whites-only party geared to reversing non-white immigration and restoring the makeup of the British population prior to 1948. For more information please visit **http://bnp.org.uk/.**

Message – This is a short, snappy statement that will be the campaign's key communication tool with the public and media. The message will be the "brand" for the campaign and it should tell people who you are, what you do and how you do it. It should help to mark you out as unique.

Press Release – Opportunity for a candidate, elected/appointed officer, or political party to address the press regarding matters that affecting the constituency, election or candidacy in a manner that serves the best interest of the party.

Promise – Something you can assure will happen if you are elected / if you succeed.

Public Relations – The building and maintaining of a relationship between an organisation / group and their clients/the general public. Public relations can involve the relationships of governments, individuals, corporations, communities, etc.

Referendum – A proposed issue on the political agenda that the entire voting population either decides to accept or reject through a direct vote.

Returning Officer – The person that is in charge of overseeing elections and announcing election results, usually for one or more groups.

Representation – Representing someone or some group with the authority to speak/act on their behalf; an official or body of elected members that serve on the behalf of their constituency.

Scope – A disability organisation in England and Wales that focuses on gaining equality for disabled persons and creating a society in which they are valued and have the same human/civil rights as everyone else.

Stakeholder – Everybody who has an interest in a project, organisation or campaign – this might include young people, youth workers, teachers, schools, the Council, the media, government and adults in your community.

Strategy – This is the plan that you come up with, plotting out how you will run your campaign.

Supporter – One who shows support and favour for a particular campaign or candidate.

Tactics – The methods you use to make people aware of your campaign / get them involved.

Target – Targets are what the young person plans to achieve when doing their challenge. The targets might be a series of steps in the process needed to complete a challenge, or they might identify particular individual goals that the young person wants to achieve.

Timetable – An organised time line, setting out deadlines, appointments and what things need to be accomplished.

UKYP - The UK Youth Parliament is a national organisation representing the views and interests of young people aged 11-18 from all over the UK. There are over 500 Members of Youth Parliament (MYPs).

War Room – A room where strategic plans/decisions are made for a campaign, typically organised to allow open communication and joint work between different sections of the campaign.

Youth Cabinet / Youth Council – A forum which represents the views of young people at a local level. Run by young people for young people, youth cabinets / councils give young people a voice, enabling them to make their views heard in the decision-making process.

Additional Information

ADDITIONAL INFORMATION

WHERE TO GO FOR FURTHER SUPPORT

ASDAN

External accrediting body for the Youth Challenges and Youth Achievement Awards.

www.asdan.co.uk

British Youth Council

The British Youth Council (BYC) is a national youth council made up of young people in youth organisations and local youth councils. They seek to represent the views of young people to government and decision makers. They promote active citizenship and campaign to ensure that all young people can fully participate in society.

www.byc.org.uk

Children's Rights Alliance for England

An alliance of over 180 organisations committed to children's human rights through the fullest implementation of the UN Convention on the Rights of the Child.

www.crae.org.uk

National Children's Bureau

Promotes the interests and well being of all children and young people across every aspect of their lives.

www.ncb.org.uk

National Council for Voluntary Youth Services

The independent voice of the voluntary youth sector in England. It provides support, information and guidance to the voluntary youth sector on the development of quality youth participation practices.

www.ncyvs.org.uk

National Youth Agency

Works to advance youth work to promote young people's personal and social development and their voice, influence and place in society.

www.nya.org.uk

Qualifications and Curriculum Development Agency

www.qca.org.uk

Save the Children

Fights for children in the UK and around the world who suffer from poverty, disease, injustice and violence. Much of their work has focus on children's and young people's rights.

www.savethechildren.org.uk

Sheila McKechnie Foundation (SMK)

The Sheila McKechnie Foundation – SMK – is a charity which works to develop a new generation of campaigners who are working to create positive and lasting social change. It offers advice and support and provides a place to share information on key areas of effective campaigning.

www.sheilamckechnie.org.uk

The Children's Society

Works with marginalised children and young people, focusing on tackling the root causes of the problems they face.

www.childrenssociety.org.ukA

UK Youth

UK Youth develops and promotes innovative non-formal education programmes and opportunities for and with young people in order to develop their full potential.

www.ukyouth.org

UK Youth Parliament

The UK Youth Parliament is a national organisation representing the views and interests of young people aged 11-18 from all over the UK.

www.ukyp.org.uk

REFERENCE

Levels of Engagement

Activity	Bronze/Youth Challenge Activities	Silver/Youth Challenge Extra	Gold
Introduction to Campaigning			
Take part in the What is a Campaign? Exercise	✓		
Take part in the Getting Your Voice Heard exercise	✓		
Participate in a discussion about why it's important for young people to get involved in campaigns	✓		
Take part in the Have YOUR say exercise	✓		
Watch a short film made by a campaign group and take part in a discussion about what defines their campaign	✓		
Take part in a workshop run by a campaign group	✓		
Help to run the What is a Campaign? exercise		✓	
Help facilitate the Getting Your Voice Heard exercise		✓	
Help plan and lead a discussion about why it's important for young people to get involved in campaigns		✓	
Help facilitate the Have YOUR say exercise		✓	
Find a campaign film for the group to watch and help to facilitate a discussion about it.		✓	
Do some research into campaign groups who could deliver a workshop.		✓	
Facilitate the What is a Campaign? Exercise			✓
Lead the Getting Your Voice Heard exercise			✓
Plan and facilitate a discussion about why it's important for young people to get involved in campaigns			✓
Design some statements for and lead the Have YOUR say exercise			✓
Plan and facilitate a discussion based around a campaign film.			✓
Research facts and information about young people's involvement in campaigns and where they have made a difference. Plan and lead a session on this.			✓
Organise for a speaker from a campaign group to deliver a workshop and chair the workshop.			✓
Planning a Campaign			
Make a list of all the issues that concern you about your community / the things that affect your life	✓		
Take part in the defining the issue exercise	✓		
Talk to other young people about how they feel about your campaign issue and record their views	✓		
Take part in a quiz on how to plan a good campaign	✓		
Take part in the choosing a campaign goal exercise	✓		
Take part in an activity taking pictures of your local community and using these as evidence to support your campaign arguments	✓		
Take part in the steps to the future exercise	✓		
Take part in an activity to research arguments for and against your campaign issue	✓		
Take part in the choosing your target exercise	✓		
Take part in some research to find out who makes the decisions that affect your campaign.	✓		
Take part in the deciding on your message exercise	✓		
Take part in some research to find out about slogans used by other campaigns	✓		
Take part in the what makes a good slogan exercise	✓		
Take part in the £5 note exercise	✓		
Take part in the lobbying exercise	✓		
Take part in the balloon exercise	✓		
Take part in the Planning a Campaign exercise	✓		
Join in a discussion about the different methods people can use to campaign	✓		
Take part in a discussion about how you will know if your campaign has been successful	✓		
Help facilitate the Planning a Campaign session		✓	
Help facilitate the Getting Your Voice Heard exercise		✓	
Help plan and lead a discussion about what young people can get from their involvement in campaigns		✓	
Help facilitate the Have YOUR say exercise		✓	
Interview young people about the issues that concern them about their community / the things that affect their lives		✓	
Help run a quiz about how to plan a good campaign		✓	
Co-run the defining the issue exercise		✓	
Work with other young people to support them in the choosing a campaign goal exercise		✓	
Work with other young people to compile photographic evidence of their local community to back up their campaign		✓	
Help facilitate the steps to the future exercise		✓	
Work with other young people to research arguments for and against your campaign issue		✓	
Co-run the choosing your target exercise		✓	
Work with other young people to research who makes the decisions that affect the campaign		✓	
Help facilitate the deciding on your message exercise		✓	
Help other young people with research on effective campaign messages		✓	
Co-facilitate the what makes a good slogan exercise		✓	
Co-facilitate the £5 note exercise		✓	
Help run the lobbying exercise		✓	
Write a letter to a local decision-maker		✓	
Co-facilitate the balloon exercise		✓	
Assist with compiling a list of different methods you can use as part of your campaign		✓	
Help run the Planning a Campaign session		✓	
Assist with research into different ways you can measure the success of your campaign		✓	
Facilitate the Planning a Campaign exercise			✓
Lead the Getting Your Voice Heard exercise			✓
Plan and facilitate a discussion about what young people can get from their involvement in campaigns			✓
Plan and lead the defining the issue exercise			✓
Facilitate the campaign goal exercise			✓
Research and design a quiz on how to plan a good campaign			✓
Run the steps to the future exercise			✓
Facilitate the choosing your target exercise			✓
Produce a guide / chart for young people illustrating who has the power to make the decisions that affect their campaign			✓
Plan and lead the deciding on your message exercise			✓
Compile a file of case studies of successful campaign messages			✓
Lead the what makes a good slogan exercise			✓
Plan and lead the £5 note exercise			✓
Plan and run the lobbying exercise			✓
Organise a letter-writing campaign to a relevant decision maker			✓
Arrange a meeting with a decision-maker			✓
Lead the balloon exercise			✓
Design some case studies on how to choose the appropriate campaign methods and plan and deliver a session with young people using these case studies.			✓
Research and compile a folder of evidence to support your campaign aim and objectives			✓
Produce a guide on the most useful websites young people can use to research arguments for and against their campaign			✓
Design a series of evaluation exercises to help measure the progress of the campaign			✓

ukyouth Hearing Unheard Voices

Levels of Engagement

Doing it!

Activity	Bronze/Youth Challenge Activities	Silver/Youth Challenge Extra	Gold
Take part in the team building exercise	✓		
Take part in a discussion about why you want to get involved in the campaign	✓		
Take part in the what I want to achieve exercise	✓		
Take part in a discussion about what you can bring to the campaign and what support you might need to get the most out of it	✓		
Take part in a workshop to design a leaflet / poster	✓		
Hand out leaflets / posters	✓		
Help get people to fill out surveys	✓		
Take part in a photo opportunity	✓		
Take part in a day of action	✓		
Take photographs of your community / what it is you want to change	✓		
Attend a song writing / poetry workshop	✓		
Take part in a drama workshop to explore your campaign issue	✓		
Help out on a stall at a conference to promote your campaign	✓		
Encourage people to sign a petition backing your campaign	✓		
Learn how to set up a campaign Facebook page	✓		
Take part in the how to create an online survey exercise	✓		
Learn about what a blog is	✓		
Take part in a demonstration / protest as part of your campaign	✓		
Take part in session to learn how to set a petition on Number 10 website	✓		
Join a relevant club at school / college	✓		
Attend a public meeting	✓		
Take part in the negotiating skills exercise	✓		
Take part in a workshop learning about how to lobby people in power	✓		
Help organise the team building exercise		✓	
Help lead a discussion about why young people want to get involved in the campaign		✓	
Support other young people to take part in the what I want to achieve exercise		✓	
Help facilitate a discussion about what young people can bring to the campaign and what support they might need to get the most out of it		✓	
Help plan a workshop to design a leaflet / poster		✓	
Help organise a rota for young people to hand out leaflets / posters		✓	
Help design a survey for young people to use		✓	
Help set up a photo opportunity		✓	
Help plan a day of action		✓	
Work with other young people to take photographs of your community / what it is you want to change		✓	
Help plan and co-facilitate a song writing / poetry workshop		✓	
Help plan a drama workshop to explore the campaign issue in a safe way		✓	
Organise a stall at a conference to promote your campaign		✓	
Set up an online petition backing your campaign		✓	
Work with other young people to set up a Facebook cause and recruit 20 members		✓	
Help to design an online survey		✓	
Work with other young people to set up a campaign blog		✓	
Help set up a relevant club / society at school or college		✓	
Help plan a demonstration / protest as part of your campaign		✓	
Help to facilitate the negotiating exercise		✓	
Help to organise a public meeting, including inviting key decision makers		✓	
Help to plan and lead a workshop learning about how to lobby people in power		✓	
Write a letter to your local councillor / MP		✓	
Plan a series of team-building activities to support young people to work better together as a group			✓
Plan and lead a discussion about why young people want to get involved in the campaign			✓
Lead the I want to achieve exercise			✓
Plan and lead a discussion about what young people can bring to the campaign and what support they might need to get the most out of it			✓
Plan and lead a workshop to design a leaflet / poster			✓
Design a survey for young people to use			✓
Liaise with local / national media to set up a photo opportunity			✓
Organise a day of action in your local community / college			✓
Plan and lead a project with other young people to collect photographic / video evidence as part of your campaign			✓
Plan and facilitate a song writing / poetry workshop			✓
Organise a drama workshop to explore the campaign issue in a safe way			✓
Set up and run a stall at a conference to promote your campaign			✓
Design and promote a petition backing your campaign			✓
Set up and manage a campaign Facebook / web page			✓
Design, promote and collate an online survey			✓
Manage a campaign blog			✓
Set up and run a relevant club or society at your school / college			✓
Plan and organise a demonstration / protest as part of your campaign, including researching what the legal situation is, approaching the appropriate authorities and negotiating with them.			✓
Plan and lead the negotiating exercise.			✓
Plan and organise a public meeting.			✓
Research, plan and lead a workshop on how to lobby people in power			✓
Organise a letter writing campaign to your local councillors / MP			✓

Shout About It!

Activity	Bronze/Youth Challenge Activities	Silver/Youth Challenge Extra	Gold
Take part in a discussion about how young people are represented in the media.	✓		
Talk to other young people about how they think they are represented in the media.	✓		
Take part in a research exercise to find out how young people are represented – collect newspaper, magazine articles, look at newspaper websites, the bbc etc.	✓		
Take part in the exercise on dealing with the media	✓		
Attend a workshop on presentation skills	✓		
Attend a talk by someone involved in your campaign	✓		
Take part in a discussion about the pros and cons of involving celebrities in your campaign	✓		
Take part in an exercise to decide who you could approach to back your campaign	✓		
Take part in a letter-writing exercise to a celebrity	✓		
Help plan and facilitate a discussion about how young people are represented in the media.		✓	
Help design a survey to find out how other young people think they are represented in the media.		✓	
Compile an evidence file on how young people are represented – collect newspaper, magazine articles, look at newspaper websites, the bbc etc.		✓	
Help to lead on the exercise on dealing with the media		✓	
Help to plan a workshop on presentation skills		✓	
Plan a talk on your campaign issue		✓	
Help plan and facilitate a discussion about the pros and cons of involving celebrities in your campaign		✓	
Help to design an exercise to decide who you could approach to back your campaign		✓	
Help lead a letter-writing exercise to a celebrity		✓	
Plan and lead a discussion about how young people are represented in the media.			✓
Research, design and co-ordinate a survey to find out how other young people think they are represented in the media.			✓
Collect evidence on how young people are represented in the media and use it to design a quiz / some case studies for use with other young people.			✓
Plan and lead the exercise on dealing with the media			✓
Plan and lead a workshop on presentation skills			✓
Research, plan and deliver a presentation on your campaign issue			✓
Research and lead a discussion about the pros and cons of involving celebrities in your campaign			✓
Collect examples of celebrities who are associated with campaigns and lead a discussion on how well these have worked.			✓
Design and run an exercise to decide who you could approach to back your campaign			✓
Run a letter-writing exercise to a celebrity with other young people			✓

Additional Information

www.ingramcontent.com/pod-product-compliance
Lightning Source LLC
Chambersburg PA
CBHW081348160426
43202CB00016B/2917